THE SEA

PETER CARTER

HEINEMANN
SP TLIGHTS

Heinemann Educational Books

Heinemann Educational Books Ltd
22 Bedford Square, London WC1B 3HH

LONDON   EDINBURGH   MELBOURNE   AUCKLAND
HONG KONG   SINGAPORE   KUALA LUMPUR
NEW DELHI   NAIROBI   JOHANNESBURG   IBADAN
KINGSTON   PORTSMOUTH (NH)

ISBN 0 435 23150 2

Typeset by The Castlefield Press of Wellingborough
Printed and bound in Great Britain by
J.W. Arrowsmith Ltd, Bristol and London

INTRODUCTION

The Sea Green Man is based on events which took place in Burford, Oxfordshire, during the third week of May, 1649, where a body of cavalry of the New Model Army was captured by Cromwell and charged with mutiny. After some hesitation on the part of Cromwell, who at first intended to shoot one in ten of the mutineers, three soldiers, Cornet Thompson and Corporals Church and Perkins, were executed by firing squad in Burford churchyard. It is a matter of record that they were defiant to the last.

The New Model Army had been created by Parliament after the Battle of Marston Moor in 1644. It was an army of a type new to England; trained and equipped to a professional standard and, in theory at least, paid on a regular basis. Its command structure was also new. Promotion from the ranks was actively encouraged by Generals such as Cromwell and Ireton.

The Civil War had various causes but the aim of the rebels was to state the supremacy of Parliament over the King's claim, founded on the theory of 'Divine Right', that he was the supreme and unchallengeable ruler of the Kingdom. Once this aim had been achieved the leaders of the Rebellion were content.

However, as is commonly the case with war, the conflict created a ferment of debate over the nature of society itself. The execution of the King, which to the Regicides was a pragmatic action, was widely seen as having symbolic significance. If the King, the personification of the property values which under-pinned English society, could be overthrown, then the values themselves were open to question.

1

The great debates during and after the Civil War borrowed religious terminology. This language, remote though it might seem today, was used to discuss real issues: in whom was ownership of the land truly vested – and why? To what extent should Parliament be representative of the people as a whole – and how? How far should religious toleration be extended? What was the role and status of women? The fact that visionary terms were employed should not blind us to the fact that they were describing matters of immediate and earthly importance.

A civil war is an expression of a nation in crisis, and such crises are marked by a proliferation of political parties as in Germany during the nineteen-twenties or in Spain during its Civil War. Political parties as we know them did not exist in the seventeenth century, but the innumerable sects, of which Richards complains in act one, scene 4, played a similar role. Many of these sects, although interesting and, indeed, admirable in their way can be dismissed as marginal to the main issues confronting the Common Wealth. However, this cannot be said of the Leveller movement.

First, the Levellers had a firm and realistic grasp of the issues, as we can see from their various pamphlets, and secondly, they had a formidable power base in the New Model Army itself. As in the British Army during the Second World War, the Civil War had led to a heightening of political consciousness among the rank and file; in addition successful experience of command in battle had given a new self-confidence to men previously kept firmly in their place.

Furthermore, political structures had developed in the army, as exemplified by the 'agitators', of whom Corporal Ward was one. These agitators were, in fact, political commissars such as are still to be found in the Soviet Red Army; the difference being, of course, that they were an expression of the will of the rank and file and not impositions upon them by a ruling political party.

The agitators were articulate, self-confident, and radical. In 1647, in co-operation with the civilian Levellers, they drew up an 'Agreement of the People', a political manifesto and Bill of

Rights. The Agreement was debated in Putney Church in 1647, by representatives of the Army in the presence of Generals Fairfax and Ireton. (The reports of the debates make fascinating reading.) Although agreement was reached on various issues, the sticking point was the refusal of the Generals to concede the Parliamentary vote to men without property. However, it was agreed to hold a general rendezvous of the entire army at some later date at which the Agreement itself could be put to the vote. This rendezvous was never held and the breaking of their promise by the Generals was a source of great bitterness among the Leveller soldiers. As Corporal Ward says in act two, scene 8 'They kept not their covenant with us.'

With the King still at large the New Model Army, with its stiffening of first-class Leveller troops, was still necessary to Parliament. Following the execution of Charles in 1649 a deliberate attempt was made to break up the Leveller regiments while retaining a formidable army which would be an obedient tool of the State. In other words, a politically conscious and radical army with high ethical standards was to be replaced by a professional mercenary army, a development regarded with horror by both Leveller troops and civilians alike.

After the King's execution it was decided to send the Army to Ireland to put down the Catholic rebellion there. Regiments for the expedition were chosen by lot. Men who, quite legally, refused to go were summarily dismissed without, it should be noted, the back pay owing to them.

Among the regiments chosen to go to Ireland were Scroope's Regiment of Horse, and Reynold's Horse. Large numbers of men in these regiments refused both to go, and to accept dismissal from what they regarded as *their* army. They were threatened with confiscation of their horses which were their own property – and valuable property at that. Against the wider background of discontent, this threat was the spark for the mutinies which took place. A somewhat shadowy agreement was made among the mutinous regiments to meet together.

The Leveller troopers from Reynold's Horse, led by Captain

William Thompson, moved through Oxfordshire while attempting to negotiate with General Fairfax, and being assured by Cromwell himself that they would not be attacked. They arrived in Burford where, with a typical lightning strike, Cromwell attacked them on the night of May 14th. 340 prisoners were taken and some 500 men made their various ways home.

Burford marked the end of the effective Leveller movement. Cromwell took the rest of the New Model Army to Ireland and, fulfilling the worst Leveller fears, waged a ferocious and merciless campaign against the Irish 'rebels', leaving a legacy of hatred which encumbers us to this day.

The Leveller movement was defeated, but the seeds sown by them, and the Diggers, and many of the other groups and sects, have continued to bear fruit. Claims made then which seemed preposterous, such as universal suffrage, are now taken for granted; other issues, such as ownership of the means of production, are very much alive.

However, although I hope that *The Sea Green Man* will stimulate discussion, I hope more that it will make the audience aware of the debt we owe to such stalwarts as Corporal Ward represents here, and to such men and women, often despised and hated as mad or trouble-makers, as Tyler and his daughter. To use their own Biblical language they were, 'Stiff-necked in the House of Rimmon and would not bow down.' They are worthy of our regard and from their overwhelming defeat have come our partial victories.

Combs,
Derbyshire.

CHARACTERS

Anyone is free to interpret the characters in the play as they wish, but the following notes might be of interest.

Tyler is meant to be admirable rather than likeable but his particular type of cranky fanaticism has been important to radicalism. He is best envisaged as a cross between a Jehovah's Witness and the early working-class members of the Labour Party. He has a prophetic vision so powerful that he is prepared to face any persecution and ridicule in order to give voice to it. Intellectual isolation, ridicule by the ignorant, and the enmity of the powerful are merely fuel for his beliefs. Whether one would choose such a man for one's own father is problematic; that we owe men like him a debt is incontestable.

That he is a cobbler is not unintentional. Until wiped out by mass-production, the term village cobbler was almost a synonym for 'radical'. Their possession of a vital skill, allied to the fact that they required little in the way of capital, gave them an independence not easily found in rural England until our own times.

I have referred to the Jehovah's Witnesses and everyone will be familiar with the sight of a Witness on their doorstep, usually accompanied by a child or an adolescent. Quite what goes on inside the heads of these Junior Witnesses, if I might describe them so, I do not know, but **Joan** should have some of their slightly eerie quality. I say 'some of' because Joan is a spirited girl, ready, able, and willing to strike back at her enemies if she has the chance, and well aware of what one might term 'Women's Liberation'.

This is not an anachronism. Women's rights to vote, to inherit, to preach were hotly debated among the dissenters of the times and the women themselves were highly organised. In 1649 *ten thousand* women signed a petition calling for the release of Leveller prisoners and the petition was presented to the House of Commons by one thousand women, wearing green ribbons.

However, advanced though Joan's views might be, she is still a child and her independence and defiance when away from her father should have just those qualities of youthful rebellion which so incenses Richards – and a great many parents today.

The Soldiers

When recruiting for his 'Ironsides' Cromwell looked for 'Men as had the fear of God in them and made some conscience of what they did.' **Ward** is the very type of such men who were the backbone of the New Model Army and, much to Cromwell's discomfiture, the Leveller movement also. Intelligent and sensible he lacks Tyler's easy fanaticism and glibness, but he is utterly loyal to his beliefs, as were Corporals Perkins and Church who met their deaths with unblinking fortitude. He is a corporal because there were no sergeants in the cavalry, a tradition still maintained in the Life Guards.

The other troopers in the play deserve a note. **Fallon** and **Gray** are not cowards. Even its enemies did not charge the New Model Army with cowardice. But they are not heroes, either. To say this is not to condemn them, heroes do not grow on every bush. They are merely frightened men who have reached their breaking point and who know very well that they are beaten. They are typical of the hundreds of their comrades who dragged their way home after Cromwell's onslaught – and dragged their way into oblivion it might be thought, but this is not necessarily so. People who have been defeated in a noble cause may turn to cynicism and pessimism. Others are not so easily deflected from their ideals and it might well be that men such as Gray and Fallon kept alive the spirit of free-thinking radicalism which was to rise again in nineteenth-century England.

The young officer **Haslam** – a cornet, that is a second lieutenant – is, by his lights, a good officer; polite but ready to use force when ordered to do so. He is in very much the same position as a subaltern in the British Army 'lifting' suspects in Northern Ireland today. He is doing a distasteful task with as little unpleasantness as possible, genuinely trying to be reasonable but ready to shoot you dead, too.

Stocks is the sort of regular soldier common to all armies, but the New Model was not a normal army. It became something more like a gigantic, armed debating society and it was of the utmost importance to the High Command and to Parliament that men such as Stocks should be kept loyal. Consequently, although he has little to say, his reactions to the discussions in the play are very important, as Haslam knows, and his acts of minor disobedience and his sparse comments should be played for all they are worth.

In the 1920s Stanley Baldwin referred, cuttingly, to a certain type of business man as 'hard-faced men who have done well out of the War.' **Richards** is such a man. However, just as Tyler should not be seen as a melodramatic hero, neither should Richards be seen as a melodramatic villain. By his standards he behaves reasonably. Since Parliament has allowed religious dissent he has not attempted to stop Tyler preaching. As far as he is concerned, Tyler can preach of the New Zion until he is blue in the face. However, when Tyler attacks property rights, and when behind him there is a formidable armed force, Richards' tolerance of free speech comes to an abrupt end. It is a commonplace of history that the solitary eccentric is tolerated but, when he acquires a following, ceases to be eccentric and becomes a menace to the established social order, he is dealt with summarily. After all, it was not until Jesus entered Jerusalem to the hosannas of the population that the plot to kill him was hatched.

So Richards deals with Tyler, but even then he operates within certain limits. Tyler is beaten up, but not seriously; Joan is thrashed, but it is Richards who halts the whipping. He makes a characteristically business-like offer to care for Tyler's goods following the eviction, although he does not offer to shelter the two human beings. He is a man of his time (he does believe Joan has a devil in her) but he is also a representative of a class which gained power after the Civil War and which still holds it in its capable hands today.

The other characters need little comment. **Francis** is a typical spoiled brat, possessing in full measure the malice such children seem peculiarly prone to. **Grote** is a bucolic idiot of a type still too common, **Pyke** a bully, subservient to his 'betters' and brutal to everyone else. **Mrs Webb** and the **Housekeeper** speak for themselves, but **the friendly neighbour** deserves a word more. Given the circumstances it is an act of great courage to help Tyler. Furthermore he is level-headed and his remarks about Joan are justified. But it is for the reader to make the choice between commonsense and fanaticism and to wonder whether, perhaps, Tyler might just be, in fact, on the road to glory.

PRODUCTION NOTES

There are sixteen important speaking parts in *The Sea Green Man* but some of these parts could be doubled, Pyke playing Stocks, the Housekeeper playing Mrs Webb, and so on. However, a shortage of actors is rarely a problem in amateur drama, particularly in school productions, and there is scope in the crowd scenes for the use of as many, or as few, extras as there are aspirant actors, and volunteers willing to make costumes.

I have tried to bear in mind the problems posed by both the arena stage and the proscenium stage. The arena stage raises few difficulties; the imaginative use of lighting, colour, sound effects, and symbolic props will be sufficient to catch the appropriate mood of the scenes.

The conventional stage raises other problems. The conventional stage and the conventional play go hand in hand. There can be one set, as in *Huis Clos*, or many sets changing between acts. *The Sea Green Man* is rather more fluid but it is structured in such a way that where set changes might be thought necessary scenes can be played in front of the curtain while these take place. For instance, Joan's encounter with Grote can be played in front of the curtain (with suitable sinister lighting) while the set is changed from Richards' kitchen to the Lock-up.

Should sets be used, there are three interiors: Tyler's cottage, Richards' kitchen, and the Lock-up. In my own experience of drama there is a great deal of fun and interest in 'back-stage' work and the making of sets and costumes can involve a whole school in creative activity in which every pupil can feel involved and rewarded, quite apart from the interest in history which such work can arouse.

However, there is no necessity for elaborate sets. By the simple replacement of props, the sets for Tyler's cottage and Richards' kitchen need not be broken down. The Lock-up presents another problem as it is necessary to see both sides of the bars. However, this can be done simply enough by the use of alternate lighting.

The other production problem is the shooting of the mutineers. Should this seem intractable there would be no objection to cutting the actual shooting and merely seeing Tyler, Joan, and Kemp kneeling as the shots ring out. But, used as we all are now to the vivid cross-cutting in film and television, spot lighting or the use of huge shadows would, I imagine, be acceptable. Of course, and better still, if the technical resources will stretch to it, the use of film can have great impact as in the original Berlin production of Brecht's *The Threepenny Opera* when Lottie Lenya, singing 'Mack the Knife' reached the lines, 'But there's someone, round the corner,' behind her on screen was film of Hitler.

But these remarks are only suggestions. Each producer will find his or her solution to the problems, such as they are.

CAST IN ORDER OF APPEARANCE

TROOPER GRAY
CORPORAL WARD
TROOPER FALLON
JOHN TYLER
JOAN TYLER
GROTE
CAPTAIN THOMPSON
PYKE
RICHARDS
FRANCIS RICHARDS
MRS GROTE
MISTRESS PRATT (Housekeeper for Richards)
CORNET HASLAM
TROOPER STOCKS
MRS WEBB
KEMP
Others: troopers, villagers, Richards' men

ACT ONE

Scene 1

Country sounds. An air of sleepy tranquillity. Enter WARD, GRAY, *and* FALLON *in the armour of the New Model Army. They wear conspicuous green ribbons but should bring with them an air of menace. They peer into the distance.*

GRAY: Is that Burford, Corporal?
WARD: That's it. Spot anything?
GRAY: No.
WARD: Fallon?
FALLON: No.
WARD: Good. Sunday morning and as quiet as a mouse. Gray!
GRAY: Corporal?
WARD: Get back and tell the Captain he can bring up the troop.

    GRAY *hesitates. Clearly he is apprehensive.*

WARD *(not too abruptly)*: Go on, man. No one is going to bite you.
GRAY: But . . .
WARD: There are no other troops within forty miles.

    GRAY *is still hesitant.*

WARD *(a little amused)*: Go with him Fallon. Hold his hand.
GRAY *(aggrieved)*: I'm not afraid.
WARD: No? You must be the only soldier who ever lived who isn't.
FALLON: Will you be all right, Corporal?

WARD *(very tough and confident, slaps his sword)*: As right as I'll
ever be. Off you go.

> GRAY *and* FALLON *exit as the church bells of Burford begin to
peal.*

Scene 2

The same Sunday morning. The interior of TYLER's *cottage. We can
hear the distinctive peal of the Burford church bells.* TYLER *is sombre
in Puritan black and wearing a tall hat.* JOAN *is in black but wearing
a white mob-cap and collar. Both give an appearance of immaculate
cleanliness. Both carry Bibles.*

TYLER: You are ready, daughter?
JOAN: Yes, father.
TYLER: Then let us set to our work of salvation.

> *They go to the front door when, without knocking,* GROTE *barges
in through the back. He is dirty and dishevelled and carrying a jug.*

TYLER *(sharp)*: What do you want, Grote?
GROTE *(grovelling)*: Morning Mister Tyler. The Missus
wondered if you could let her have some milk. We've run out.
TYLER: Again. Oh, very well. Joan?

> JOAN *pours out milk.*

GROTE: You going out on that preaching, then?
TYLER: It's Sunday, isn't it?
GROTE: Course it is. You can hear the bells can't you? Where be
you preaching?
TYLER: At the market cross.
GROTE: You should be in church, that's where you should be,
listening to the Parson.
TYLER: Why should I listen to him?
GROTE: Well, he's paid to, isn't he? Paid to preach, like.
TYLER: Yes, paid to tell us what our masters want us to hear.

GROTE *(vaguely)*: Ah . . . you'll get into trouble, you will.

TYLER: Every man is free to preach. Cromwell and Parliament have said so.

GROTE *(shrewdly)*: Don't know about that but it ain't Parliament what rules the roost round here, it's Master Richards and Master Coles.

TYLER *makes a contemptuous gesture.*

GROTE: It's all right being like that but they're the gaffers. Own everything round here they do.

TYLER: He doesn't own me, or this house. I am my own man.

GROTE: It's all right for some, but you'll get us all into trouble. I'm telling you, Master Richards don't like it.

TYLER: Man is born to trouble as the sparks fly upwards. You have your milk.

GROTE *(peers vaguely into the jug)*: Oh, ah.

TYLER: Then good day to you.

GROTE: Ah. *(shambles out, pauses)* Er, have you got a bit of bread?

TYLER *(suppressing irritation)*: Here man. *(Gives GROTE a chunk and firmly pushes him out.)* A creature who walks in darkness. As if I would let one such as Richards prevent me from doing the Lord's work, and on the Sabbath. So, come Joan, I feel the hand of the Lord is with us this day.

Both exit.

Scene 3

As scene 1. Church bells still ringing. WARD on stage. The stage gradually filling with troopers of the New Model Army, all wearing green ribbons. GRAY, FALLON, and THOMPSON prominent.

WARD *(raising his hand in salute)*: Captain.

THOMPSON: All in order?

WARD: Yes. All's quiet.

THOMPSON: Good. *(faces his men)* Comrades, that town is

Burford. We are going to take it and stay overnight. Remember, strict discipline. No-one and nothing is to be harmed. Not a man nor a woman nor a child, neither bird nor beast. Is that understood?

A chorus of assent but one voice is raised.

VOICE: Captain Thompson!

THOMPSON: Yes? Speak up that man.

VOICE *(ruefully)*: We've got to eat and drink, Captain. *(murmur of assent)* And I've got no money!

Good natured laughter and shouts of: Neither have I. What's money?

THOMPSON: Understood. Give a warrant for anything you need. I will guarantee them. That means cheese and ale, not beef and wine.

More laughter.

THOMPSON: So. Swords out!

An ominous rattle as the swords are unsheathed. Helmets adjusted, etc. The mood changes from good humour to menacing seriousness.

THOMPSON: So! God with us. Corporal Ward, lead the way!

Led by WARD, GRAY *and* FALLON, *all exit.*

Scene 4

Richards' yard. The bells ringing. Various servants lounging about dressed in what passes for their Sunday best. PYKE, *with a stout stick, prominent.*
    Enter RICHARDS *and* FRANCIS. *Instant subservience: hats doffed, forelocks tugged, curtsies, etc.*

RICHARDS: Are your souls ready to hear divine service?

Deferential assent; Aye Master, Yes Sir, *etc.*

PYKE: All ready, Sir.

RICHARDS: Good. Bring the horses.

PYKE *(shouts over his shoulder)*: Clegg! *(CLEGG slouches off stage.)* Master Richards.

RICHARDS: What is it?

PYKE: It's John Tyler, Master, the cobbler.

RICHARDS: That dog. What of him?

PYKE: He's going to preach today, Sir, at the market cross.

RICHARDS: So he does every Sunday.

PYKE: Aye, but today he's going to preach on something different.

RICHARDS: Different? *(sharply)* How different?

PYKE: They say he's going to preach about the common lands, Sir.

RICHARDS: What!

PYKE: It's true, Master. All the town knows of it. He says that you took the commons off the people.

FRANCIS *(approaches ingratiatingly)*: What is it, Father?

RICHARDS *(enraged)*: Tyler! An ignorant cobbler! He says that I stole the commons!

FRANCIS *(hideously sycophantic)*: You didn't steal them.

RICHARDS: Indeed I did not. I enclosed them under the law of the land.

PYKE: Master Coles had trouble on his estate, Sir. Some rascals came and said it was common land. They drove his sheep off and planted vegetables.

RICHARDS: I know those dogs. Diggers they call themselves. *(anger mounting)* I paid for three men to fight for Parliament against the King and what has happened? Every scoundrel in England thinks he is the equal of his betters! Diggers, Levellers, Ranters, Fifth Monarchy men! Hordes of the ruffians wandering about and all demanding a say in the ruling of the country!

FRANCIS *(loathsome precosity)*: Some of them refuse to take their hats off to me, Father.

RICHARDS: I'd have their heads off!

PYKE: What has happened to law and order, Master?

RICHARDS: I wonder. Did we kill a king for this? Now the lid is off the pot.

PYKE: And there is a witches' brew boiling.

RICHARDS *(grimly)*: We'll quench that fire. *(Takes PYKE aside.)* I don't want Tyler preaching again.

PYKE: No, Master.

RICHARDS: You know what to do.

PYKE *(with relish)*: I do. *(Slams his club against his hand.)*

RICHARDS: Not that! I don't want anyone killed. But teach the dog a lesson.

PYKE: A lesson. Right, Master.

RICHARDS: One he won't forget, or those who listen to him.

PYKE: We'll deal with him.

RICHARDS: See that you do. Take the men. They will have to miss church. Francis, come. Time for divine service.

RICHARDS, FRANCIS, *and the* WOMEN *move off stage as* PYKE *is collecting his* MEN.

RICHARDS *(turning)*: Deal with him!

The church bells stop abruptly.

Scene 5

The same Sunday.

The market cross in Burford. TYLER *and* JOAN *are standing on the steps of the cross. They have a small, docile* AUDIENCE. TYLER *is wearing his tall hat and holding his Bible which has a distinctive green book mark.* JOAN, *immaculate, is standing with him with her Bible. Apart from the* AUDIENCE, *there are* PASSERS-BY *on their way to church.*

TYLER *(his voice raised, addressing the* PASSERS-BY*)*: Brothers and Sisters, hear the word of the Lord! Hear His word as He

spoke it, under the heavens. Hear the word of the Lord God
Almighty which was written down for all to hear! *(with relish)*
My text is Chapter nineteen, Verse ten, of the Book called
Deuteronomy.

VOICE: Duty what?

> *The crowd laugh.*

TYLER *(solemnly)*: That is the Fifth Book of Moses! Moses! He
who led the Children of Israel from the bondage of Egypt and
from under the heel of Pharoah, and into the Promised Land!

> *Recognising at least the word Moses, the* CROWD *relapses into a
respectful silence.*

TYLER *(An impressive pause, then holds up his Bible and makes it
clear that he is reading aloud.)*: The word of the Lord! 'Thou shalt
not remove thy neighbour's landmark' –

> *As he speaks* PYKE *and his* MEN *infiltrate the* AUDIENCE *in a
menacing way.*

TYLER *(aware of them raises his voice defiantly)*: 'Thou shalt not
remove thy neighbour's landmark which they of old times
have set by inheritance *(very impressively)* which *thou, thou* shalt
soon inherit in the land the Lord thy God gives thee.'

PYKE *(elbowing to the front of the* CROWD*)*: You should listen to
your own words, Tyler. It's levelling dogs like you who go
around knocking down landmarks.

TYLER: Ah, Richards' echo!

PYKE *(savagely)*: I'll echo you if you aren't careful. Who knocked
down Master Coles' landmarks?

> *In the ensuing dialogue the* AUDIENCE *should be visibly moved
one way and the other. They now mutter,* That's right. Someone
did. *etc.*

TYLER: Coles set his bounds around the common land. *He*
knocked down the landmarks which our forefathers set for us.
He and Richards have enclosed land which belonged to all of

us. They have turned men off to put sheep on, and now the sheep eat up the men! *(Approval from the crowd.* TYLER *points out individuals.)* You, Mister Briggs, did you not have geese on the common? And you, Mistress Sykes, you had pigs there. Where are they now? Gone! All gone! Now you are at the landlord's beck and call and take the pittance he chooses to give you! *(Points at* PYKE, *addressing him.)* Why should men toil all day in the fields and go home hungry to a hungry house while one man toils not but eats of the fruits of the earth, growing fat selling our wheat and our wool? Is that justice?

The AUDIENCE *is swayed to* TYLER*'s side by this.*

PYKE: You are a trouble maker.
TYLER: I a trouble maker? It was not I who raised an army against King Charles. Why have we just now fought a bloody war against the King and all his cavalleros if not that we should all be equal, all men, and women, too! *(He proudly places his hand upon* JOAN*'s shoulder.)*
PYKE: How can a woman be equal? What do you know anyway, Tyler. You're just a cobbler.
TYLER: And Jesus Christ was just a carpenter! Aye, the Son of God earned his living by the sweat of his brow. And what were his Disciples but common workmen? Men like us. Yet Christ chose them above all others to follow him and to preach the Gospel to all Nations. And now we preach the true Gospel. Us! Not the Parsons who grow fat on our labour.

The CROWD *murmur approval at this popular argument.*

PYKE *(simulates outrage)*: Why, this is blasphemy!
JOAN: Blasphemy to preach the word of the Lord?
PYKE *(simulating horror)*: A woman preaching! A girl!

For reasons unclear to it, this causes unease among the CROWD.

TYLER: Why should not a woman preach as well as a man? What is there against it?
VOICE: Parson says women should keep their mouths shut in

church. He read it from the Bible book.

TYLER: We're not in church, Brother.

This feeble sally raises an appreciative guffaw from the CROWD. *Cries of:* That's a good one. He got you there, Will. *etc.*

PYKE *(feeling that he is losing he becomes more assertive)*: It's against all law of Nature. It's unnatural!

This disturbs the CROWD. *Mumbles of* Aye, 'tain't natural, *etc.*

JOAN *(boldly holds up her Bible and reads from it)*: 'And Deborah, a prophetess, the wife of Lapidon, she judged Israel at that time.'

PYKE *(taken aback)*: What's that supposed to mean?

JOAN: A woman judged all Israel, the Chosen People of God! Yes, a woman, a daughter of Eve. If she could judge Israel why should not a woman preach?

PYKE *(defeated)*: You're not a woman, you're just a girl.

TYLER: All are equal before the Throne of God.

PYKE: God! Did you hear what he said? God. Take off your hat when you say that word. You're profaning the Sabbath!

PYKE eggs on his MEN *who chant,* Uncover, uncover.

PYKE: Take off that hat!

TYLER: For Christ or for Richards? Friends –

PYKE: You've got no friends here. Agitator!

PYKE's MEN *begin to jostle the* CROWD *who, seeing that the situation is turning ugly, begin to back away.*

TYLER: I have the right to –

PYKE: You've got no rights, either. Clear off.

One of his MEN *throws a stone which hits* TYLER *in the face. More stones and rubbish follow as* TYLER *tries to speak and to defend* JOAN.

TYLER: Friends, don't let these men –

PYKE moves forward, kicks TYLER's *legs from under him, and gives him another kick for good measure.*

PYKE *(viciously)*: There's your rights. Now get off and keep your mouth shut.

    PYKE *and his* MEN *exit watched by the frightened* CROWD. JOAN *kneels and holds her dazed father.*

JOAN: Looking around. Will no one help?

    The CROWD *turns away and exits.*

JOAN: Oh, Father!

TYLER: I shall be all right, child. But now we see how the Devil stalks the land.

JOAN *(with spirit)*: I would have thrown the stones back at them.

TYLER: Richards and his kind want that, Joan. There is nothing they want more than to set the common people on each other like a dog fight.

JOAN: You hit back in the wars.

TYLER: That was different.

JOAN: How different?

TYLER *(wearily)*: Just . . . just different. We had a common cause and a clear aim.

JOAN: But why do people behave so?

TYLER: Ignorance. How many people can read? And without learning what can they know? They spend six days a week in the fields like dumb animals and on the seventh day the Parsons stuff their heads with lies.

JOAN: Animals they are.

TYLER: Well, animals . . . they are men, Daughter, with immortal souls.

    JOAN *visibly dissents, turning her head away.*

TYLER: Now Joan, they can be taught. Did you notice how they approved when I spoke of the enclosures?

JOAN: Aye, and I noticed how they approved when Pyke spoke about women, and I noticed how they refused to help you when you were kicked down.

TYLER: They were frightened of Pyke. But they will learn.

JOAN *(sharply)*: When?

TYLER: When they have responsibility. They need that. What life do they lead now? Ordered to do this and that, poked and prodded like pigs at market, and if they do open their mouths bullies like Pyke are set upon them. But I have seen men behave differently. In the army I saw common men command whole companies, yes, and regiments! And they beat their betters, whipped them from the field in battle after battle. And now, in the New Model Army, every troop elects its own agitator to speak for it, and the entire army joins in a great debate about the future of the Common Wealth. Maybe . . . if every man had a vote that would be a way forward.

JOAN: And every woman.

TYLER *(struck by this new thought)*: Why not? Why not that? The entire nation voting! Who knows then what miracles the Lord will work in England. *(He rises to his feet.)* Yes. *(He and* JOAN *take a few steps.)* The New Jerusalem.

> *They take a few more steps then halt, amazed. Facing them are* TROOPERS *of the New Model Army. They are wearing green ribbons but the effect is overwhelmingly formidable and sinister.*

TROOPER *(in an inhuman voice)*: Back!

TYLER *(raises his arms)*: Friend! Saviour!

TROOPER: Back!

TYLER: Brother, we are going home.

TROOPER: Find another way.

TYLER: Yes! Yes! *(turns to* JOAN*)* Daughter, the Lord of Hosts is with us this day!

Scene 6

Sunday. Later.

> TYLER's *cottage.* TYLER *and* JOAN *enter.*

TYLER *(in a state of exaltation)*: Now are the Prophets justified!

The Lord has answered us from the whirlwind!

Enter GROTE *and his* WIFE *and a crowd of other* NEIGHBOURS.

GROTE: Tyler, Tyler! Have you seen? The town is full of soldiers! No-one is allowed to leave!

MRS GROTE: They've taken over all the inns. Staying there, they are!

VOICE: They say that the King has come back.

MRS GROTE *(with relish)*: To punish that wicked Cromwell. *(Staring meaningfully at* TYLER*)* and all like him.

VOICE: Good King Charles back!

A general hubbub. The King! Oliver! Another war! *etc.*

TYLER: Charles back? Why then he is a second Lazarus to rise from the dead for his head is chopped off.

MRS GROTE: There be other kings.

TYLER: None in England, nor ever shall be again. And if there were these soldiers would not bring them back.

MRS GROTE *(shrewishly)*: For why? For why?

VOICE: Because these be Roundheads. Ain't that right, Mister Tyler?

TYLER: Yes, they are Roundheads. They are the army of the Common Wealth. But they are more than that.

GROTE: More than what?

TYLER: You have seen the ribbons they are wearing?

VOICE *(excited)*: I saw them. Green ribbons, all over them.

VARIOUS VOICES: I saw them. Yes. I saw them first. What are you talking about? I saw them first.

The beginning of a minor, idiotic fracas silenced by Mrs Grote's hideously penetrating voice.

MRS GROTE: All right. Green ribbons. What about them?

TYLER *(solemn and impressive)*: They are sea-green ribbons.

MRS GROTE: Sea-green ribbons?

TYLER: Aye, for these are the Sea Green Men.

A stunned silence.

GROTE *(with superstitious awe)*: Sea Green Men?

TYLER: Yes. Those who God has raised to pull down the mighty from their seats, and to exalt the poor and humble.

GROTE: What are you talking about, then?

TYLER *(triumphantly)*: These men are Levellers, and the sea-green ribbon is their emblem.

MRS GROTE: Levellers? They be soldiers. I saw them with my own eyes.

General assent.

TYLER *(impatiently)*: Of course they are soldiers, but they are soldiers of the Lord. They believe that all men should be equal.

GROTE *(stunned)*: But what will our masters say?

TYLER: There will be no more masters.

Incredulity among the NEIGHBOURS. No more masters! What about Master Richards? What will we do? *etc.*

TYLER: No more masters. No more Richards and his like! Oh, there will be a weeping and wailing and a gnashing of teeth, but the Righteous will rejoice.

GROTE *(bewildered)*: Wailing . . . teeth . . ?

MRS GROTE *(maliciously)*: You are a sea-green man!

TYLER: Have I ever denied it? Yes, I am a Leveller.

GROTE *(slowly comprehending)*: You mean that . . . you mean you're going to get rid of the Master?

TYLER: Yes. And Coles, and the Parson, and all the other buzzards who feed off us.

GROTE *(alarmed)*: I want no part in this. *(He moves to the door among a general exodus.)* You come along with me, Missis.

As he peers timidly through the door MRS GROTE *turns.*

MRS GROTE *(with real venom)*: You and your like, you want to turn the world upside down.

TYLER: We'll put it the right side up – for once.

MRS GROTE: Why don't you leave things alone? Leave us be!
Who are you, anyway? Who are you to lord it over us?

TYLER *(incredulously)*: I? I lord it over you?

MRS GROTE: You know what I mean – just because you've got
a few books –

GROTE *(reappearing at the door)*: Come on, Missis! There's
soldiers at the back.

MRS GROTE *squeals and runs to the door, turning for a parting
shot.*

MRS GROTE: You'll end up on the gallows.

TYLER *(shoving her out)*: And you'll end up . . . *(He shrugs as* MRS
GROTE *exits.)* Sheep have more sense. But the day has dawned!
Zion has come again! That I should have lived to see this day!

JOAN *(tentatively)*: Father.

TYLER: Freed from the shackles . . .

JOAN: Father.

TYLER: What?

JOAN: The men . . . the soldiers . . .

TYLER: Our deliverers!

JOAN: Yes. But we don't know why they are here, do we? We
haven't spoken to them. They might be here for anything.

TYLER: No! No! It is the new revolution. I know it! It is the Day
of Judgement and we must prepare ourselves for it. Take the
Bible, Daughter. Read me psalm ten, the 15th verse.

JOAN, *clearly not convinced that the Day of Judgement has
arrived, opens her Bible. With practised ease she finds the psalm and
reads:*

JOAN: 'Break thou the arm of the wicked and evil man –'

TYLER: Richards!

JOAN *(gives her father a penetrating stare, then resumes
reading)*: 'Seek out his wickedness till thou find none.'

TYLER *(stalking the room in exultation)*: Break the arm of the
wicked man! Break the arm of Richards and Coles. God has
sent his Sea Green Men to do that; here, in Burford! *(He strides*

to the door and looks out.)

VOICE *(harsh and soldierly)*: You there – get inside.

TYLER *(retreats into the room)*: The voice of the soldier of the Lord! Daughter, we will spend this day in fasting and prayer that the Lord Jehovah will bless our cause.

Scene 7

A room in an inn. A bed and a chair. FALLON is lying on the bed reading. GRAY is pacing restlessly about the room. Their armour is in a corner carrying prominent green ribbons.

FALLON *(irritated by GRAY)*: What's the matter with you?

GRAY: What do you think? *(peers anxiously through the window)* I hope we've plenty of guards out.

FALLON: Don't worry, Captain Thompson will have made sure of that. *(with a little difficulty he reads out loud)* 'He that kills men merely . . . because of orders . . . or . . . money is a murderer and . . . shall not escape the . . . judgement of God . . .'

GRAY *(impatiently)*: What's that you're reading?

FALLON *(holds up pamphlet)*: The English Soldier's Standard. You ought to read it.

GRAY *(bitterly)*: I've read enough to last me the rest of my life.

FALLON *(swings legs off bed and looks thoughtfully at GRAY)*: I don't understand you. *(holds up his hand pacifically)* Seriously, I don't. You wear a green ribbon but –

GRAY: But I am no true Leveller.

FALLON *(wildly)*: I didn't say that.

GRAY: No, but that's what you mean. *(He paces to the window and peers out again.)* I am a Leveller, I am! I was a chairmaker before the war. Do you think that I liked being lorded over by gentlemen and gentlewomen? And do you think I liked having to raise my hat to every spoiled brat that passed me by? It's why I joined the army in the first place. But I didn't count on this.

FALLON: This?

GRAY: Mutiny? Traipsing across half England hoping to meet

other Leveller regiments *(with a genuine frisson of horror)* with Cromwell on our heels, Cromwell! *(He stands over* FALLON.*)* I want everything you want; yes, the vote for every man, the land shared, tolerance of religion, freedom of speech. But . . .

FALLON: But?

GRAY: But I don't want to die for it. *(peers through the window again)* Burford! I'd never even heard of the place before yesterday and now –

He is cut off as WARD *enters.*

FALLON *(eagerly)*: Is everything all right?

WARD *(giving* FALLON *a hard stare)*: All right? Yes. Why shouldn't it be? Colonel Reynolds is negotiating with Cromwell.

FALLON: About what, in God's name?

WARD *(evenly)*: You know as well as I do. No man has to go to Ireland unless he volunteers. No man is discharged from the army if he refuses to go unless he gets all his back pay – and no reprisals.

GRAY: Reprisals! How did I get into this?

WARD: You had your say. You voted with the rest of us.

GRAY: Voted!

WARD *(takes* GRAY *by the shoulder. He is friendly but firm.)*: Gray, we are living like free men. That is what voting is about, choosing your own destiny. Think about that. We wear a uniform but we are not slaves, we are free men.

GRAY: We'll soon be dead men.

WARD *(very tough)*: Enough of that!

FALLON *(anxious to relieve tension)*: Corporal, what about the other regiments?

WARD: We are going to have a general rendezvous in Bristol. We get a dozen regiments together and it will be a different tale. Then we will start to make a new England. *Our* England.

GRAY: If Cromwell doesn't catch us first.

WARD: Enough of that! He won't attack us while we are negotiating. We have his word on that.

GRAY: Cromwell's word!

WARD *(sharply and showing authority)*: Yes, his word and promise. Anyway, he is in Oxford, forty miles away. He would need wings to get here before tomorrow noon and we're moving out at dawn. So turn in and get some rest. *(goes to the door)* Calm your fears. Good night. *(Exits.)*

Scene 8

Dusk. The same Sunday.

> The kitchen in RICHARDS' *house*. RICHARDS. FRANCIS. HOUSEKEEPER. PYKE. *Other* SERVANTS. *An air of panicky bustle as* SERVANTS *pack various articles, sort out food, etc.*

RICHARDS: Are all the men in their places?

PYKE: Yes, Master.

RICHARDS: And the horses, are they in?

PYKE: All stabled and guarded.

RICHARDS: Have you given out the muskets?

PYKE: All to the best shots, Sir.

RICHARDS: Good. Arm the rest with what you can find. Anything, scythes, bill-hooks. *(to HOUSEKEEPER, sharply)* Are you listing those provisions?

HOUSEKEEPER: Every loaf, Master.

PYKE: You think that there will be a siege, Sir?

RICHARDS: I don't know what's going to happen, but we'll be ready if they do attack.

FRANCIS *(snivelling with fear)*: Why are the soldiers here, Father?

RICHARDS *(exploding with rage)*: Because they are scoundrels. Mutinous dogs. The Generals of the army have ordered them to go to Ireland and they refuse to go. Refused! Soldiers refusing orders! And when they are turned out of the army they whine about the pay they say they are owed. Now they are roaming about the countryside preaching rebellion against Parliament!

FRANCIS: But are there no good soldiers?

RICHARDS *(grimly)*: Yes, and plenty of them. Go to your room.
FRANCIS *(whining)*: But will these bad soldiers kill us?
RICHARDS *(without conviction)*: No. *(bellows)* Did I tell you to get to your room?

FRANCIS *runs out.*

RICHARDS *(to* PYKE*)*: See if you can get a man through to Master Coles – and another man to the manor to see what's happening.

PYKE *hesitates.*

RICHARDS: Well?
PYKE: It might be hard to get them to go.
RICHARDS: Then put a horse whip across their backs! Get on with it.

Exit PYKE.

HOUSEKEEPER: Lord, Master, what would your dear wives have said if they had seen this?
RICHARDS: Wives? Wives? What are you babbling about them for? Get on with your work. *(He takes a pistol from a drawer, looks at it carefully, then replaces it.)*
RICHARDS *(to* SERVANTS*)*: Move! Move!

The SERVANTS *bustle about.*

Scene 9

The same Sunday. Night.

TYLER*'s cottage.* TYLER *is indefatigably reading aloud from the Bible.* JOAN *is obviously exhausted and half asleep.*

TYLER *(reading aloud)*: 'Thou hast broken Rahab in pieces, as one that is slain; thou hast scattered thine enemies with thy strong arm.' Blessed be the men who gave us the Bible in our own tongue.
JOAN *(sleepily)*: Yes, Father.

Act One

TYLER: And now a prayer.

> JOAN *wearily drags herself from her chair and kneels, her face against its seat.*

TYLER: May the hand of the Lord keep us safe from all harm this night and forever more, and may He bless the swords of the Sea Green Men. And may He strike down Richards and Coles and all evil and wicked men . . . *(He sees that JOAN is sound asleep. Hesitates, but humanity overcoming his fanaticism, murmurs)* Amen, amen, amen. *(He gently shakes JOAN.)* Daughter.

JOAN *(wakening and a little apprehensive)*: I'm sorry, Father.

TYLER: We must beware the weakness of the flesh. But . . . but it is late. So go to bed, chuck. Tomorrow will bring greater wonders.

> JOAN *bows her head as TYLER places his hand on it and blesses her.*

TYLER: The Lord bless you and keep you. Good night, child.

JOAN: Good night, Father. The Lord keep you.

> JOAN *exits.* TYLER *walks restlessly about the room. Peers through the window, then settles down with his Bible. Reads a little while. Murmurs, following the text;* 'And I saw a new heaven and a new earth . . .' *As he does so we hear the distant sounds of an affray. Musket shots, shouts, then a crash as Cromwell's cavalry thunder into Burford.* TYLER *rushes to the door and opens it. Wild shouts and screams; curses and oaths. Sounds of musketry, horses and the wild jangling of Church bells, etc.* TYLER *hastily slams the door.*
> *Enter* JOAN.

JOAN: Father! What is happening?

TYLER *(in great agitation)*: Soldiers! The army! Cromwell's men!

> *The sound of the fight contiues.*

JOAN: Cromwell?

TYLER *(in a frenzy)*: Yes! Yes!

> *A tremendous volley of musketry and wild screams outside the*

house.

TYLER: Get upstairs.

JOAN: But –

TYLER: Do as I say. Go! Stay there.

JOAN *(stoutly)*: I will stay here with you.

TYLER *(taking JOAN's arm)*: Go. *(Takes her firmly to the door.)* Stay in your room. Do not undress. These –

JOAN: These what?

TYLER *(regretting his words, mumbles)*: These are the ranks of the ungodly. Now go.

> *He shoves JOAN through the door. He moves about the room with spasmodic irresolution. Picks up his Bible, opens it, puts it down. He mutters to himself.*

TYLER: It cannot be. It cannot!

> *Finally he takes a hammer and sits down facing the door.*
> *The scene could end here, but preferably dim lights briefly showing the passage of time. Raise lights. The sound of battle is over. Dawn, cocks crowing, etc. The sinister approach of horses. A violent banging on the door.*

VOICE: Open up! *(more banging)* Open up in there!

> *TYLER wakes, startled. Tremendous banging on the door.*

TYLER *(shouts up the stairs)*: Joan! Joan! Stay where you are.

> *As the door is obviously being broken down he unbolts it. STOCKS barges in with other TROOPERS followed by HASLAM with a scroll, and RICHARDS. TYLER is knocked sprawling.*

RICHARDS *(triumphantly)*: That is the man. Take him!

ACT TWO

Scene 1

Monday, dawn.

TYLER*'s cottage.* TYLER *held by the* TROOPERS.

TYLER: What is this?

HASLAM *(looking at* TYLER*'s books with some respect)*: You are under arrest.

TYLER Arrested! Where is your warrant?

HASLAM: I need none. The town is under martial law by order of the Lord General Cromwell. Get your coat on. Move!

RICHARDS: The mutiny is crushed! Now we will put down all Leveller dogs!

HASLAM *(sharply)*: No need for that language.

TYLER: Can a man be arrested for his beliefs?

RICHARDS: No, but for raising rebellion, preaching treason, and aiding the mutineers.

TYLER: I have not left this house since yesterday morn.

HASLAM *(pointing to* TYLER*'s battered face)*: Then where did you ger those?

TYLER *(pointing at* RICHARDS*)*: Ask him.

RICHARDS: I know nothing of it –

As he speaks the door opens and JOAN *appears.*

HASLAM *(surprised)*: Who is this?

RICHARDS: A malignant brat.

TYLER: You – *(lunges forward but is restrained by the* TROOPERS*).*

33

JOAN *(defiantly)*: I am no brat.

HASLAM *(to* TYLER*)*: Your daughter?

TYLER: Yes.

HASLAM: Where is your wife?

TYLER: Dead. Dead, buried and risen to glory.

RICHARDS *(turns to* HASLAM *in disgust)*: Take them.

HASLAM *(looks at his document)*: There is nothing here about a girl.

RICHARDS: Then take the man.

HASLAM: And leave a girl alone in a town full of troops?

RICHARDS: What does that matter?

HASLAM: A lot – to me.

RICHARDS *(thinking)*: The neighbours! Leave her with them.

JOAN: I go nowhere unless my father bids me.

RICHARDS: Hear that! Did I not say she was a malignant?

TYLER: Mind your language, Richards.

RICHARDS: Insolence! Take off your hat when you speak to your betters.

TYLER: Take off yours.

HASLAM *(finding this exchange tedious)*: Watch them, Stocks. I'll see the neighbours. *(to* TYLER*)* Will you behave yourself? *(*TYLER *reluctantly nods.)* Then release him.

    HASLAM *exits as* TYLER *is released. He takes* JOAN's *hand.*

TYLER: So, you think that the hour of your triumph is come.

RICHARDS: That came when we overthrew Charles Stuart.

TYLER: We? I never saw you with a sword.

RICHARDS: It was men such as I who paid for the war.

JOAN: And it was men such as my father who fought it.

RICHARDS *(exasperated)*: Will you never stop your prattling?

STOCKS *(gruff but not unkind)*: You keep silent, Missie.

RICHARDS *(to* TYLER*)*: You fought for wages.

TYLER *(to a certain approbation from* STOCKS*)*: Not I, nor those like me. We were no mercenaries hired to kill our fellow men for money. We fought for the equality of man.

RICHARDS *(goaded)*: Equality! What would you have? The King has been executed, the Protestant religion is saved, and Parliament has triumphed, has it not?

TYLER: So they say. But is my voice heard there?

RICHARDS: I speak for you.

TYLER: You speak for me? What interests hold us together? I have more in common with a Dutch cobbler than with you.

RICHARDS: We are both Englishmen –

TYLER *(laughs)*: Beat the drum and wave the flag! Tell me another tale.

RICHARDS *(choking back his anger and attempting to wheedle)*: Tyler, you are not a stupid man, I grant you that –

TYLER *gives an ironical bow.*

RICHARDS: I mean it. You are not like the other clowns here. You can read, even. So cannot you understand that to have a say in the ruling of the land you must own property – land. What land do you have?

TYLER: None, now. But we will share it out.

RICHARDS: Steal it, you mean.

TYLER: No! We will take back what is ours by right. You are the thief. You stole it from the King's men who stole it from our Saxon forefathers who held all things in common.

RICHARDS: Tyler, there are rich men and there are poor men. There always have been and there always will be. God has ordained it so. Did not Christ say that the poor will be with us always? Dare you oppose God's will?

TYLER *(sure of himself)*: Christ meant the poor in heart – the humble folk. And he said that the poor would inherit the Kingdom of Heaven.

RICHARDS *(eagerly)*: Heaven!

TYLER: Aye, but does not Revelations tell us that there will be a new Heaven and a new Earth? *(cutting off RICHARDS' protest)* You were born naked yet now you own a thousand acres. Did God ordain that? No. You married well and you made money during the war, selling corn and wool dear and grabbing land from the King's men. Now their heel is off your neck but yours is still on mine.

RICHARDS *(playing his last card, whispers confidentially, one eye on the troopers)*: Tyler, if you would only keep your mouth shut I could do things for you. I could –

TYLER *(laughs)*: So spoke the Devil to the Christ when he tempted Him on the mountain. *(laughs again)* First you beat me, now you bribe me!

RICHARDS: It is commonsense! Listen –

He is cut off as HASLAM *enters, exasperated.*

HASLAM: None of the neighbours will take the girl. They're all frightened out of their wits.

RICHARDS: Then just take the man. You have your orders! What does she matter?

HASLAM *(outraged)*: Sir!

The TROOPERS *are as shocked as* HASLAM. *Aware of this* RICHARDS *retracts.*

RICHARDS: I didn't mean –

STOCKS: Excuse me, Sir.

HASLAM: Yes?

STOCKS: Perhaps if . . . if the gentleman took the girl.

TYLER: Never that!

He lunges forward but is rammed, expertly, against the wall by STOCKS.

STOCKS *(twisting* TYLER's *arm)*: You just calm down or –

JOAN: Father!

She runs forward but is held by a TROOPER.

TROOPER *(not unkindly)*: Now, now, Miss.

HASLAM *(in irritation to* RICHARDS*)*: Will you take her or not?

RICHARDS *(equally cross)*: Very well. But I will have a word with your Captain about this.

HASLAM: Speak to General Cromwell if you wish. Right. Bring that man.

TYLER *(as he is marched to the door)*: You will pay for this, Richards.

HASLAM: That's enough.

TYLER: I suppose I might say goodbye to my child?

HASLAM: Of course. But behave yourself.

> TYLER *kisses* JOAN.

TYLER: Do not be afraid, Joan. The arm of the Lord will defend us both. *(to* RICHARDS*)* I hold you responsible for her well being.

HASLAM: Out!

> HASLAM, TYLER, *and the* TROOPERS *exit.*

RICHARDS *(impatiently)*: Come along, you.

JOAN *(bold defiance)*: I suppose I may take my Bible.

RICHARDS: Do you take me for a monster?

JOAN *(taking her Bible)*: Do you take yourself for a man?

> RICHARDS, *enraged, raises his hand to strike* JOAN *but lowers it.*

RICHARDS: Out!

Scene 2

A wood or copse. The following Wednesday.

> *Enter* WARD, FALLON *and* GRAY. *They are exhausted and dishevelled although they are still wearing their green ribbons.* WARD *is wounded and slumps to the ground.*

GRAY *(throws off his helmet)*: Sweet Jesus!

FALLON: Let me look at that wound, Corporal. *(looks)* It's a bad gash.

WARD *(in pain but making light of his injury)*: It's just a scratch. We were lucky.

FALLON: Lucky!

WARD: We got away, didn't we?

FALLON *(pours wine over* WARD's *wound.* WARD *winces)*: Sorry. *(half admiringly)* That was some gallop Cromwell made, though. Forty miles . . .

WARD *(with pride)*: Roundhead cavalry.

GRAY: What is this? We've been hunted like hares for two days and you are talking about how good the cavalry is. You'll be writing Cromwell a letter of congratulations next.

Throughout the next speeches GRAY *takes off his armour.*

WARD: Easy, Brother.

GRAY *(bitterly)*: It was easy for them. Four hundred of us and how many got away?

WARD: Maybe more than you think. And when we get together –

GRAY: We'll have a party! Christ, I should have gone to Ireland. Orders are orders.

WARD: It depends on the orders. If you were told to –

He is cut off as GRAY *leaps to his feet and holds up a warning finger. A tense moment and then* GRAY *relaxes.*

GRAY: I thought that I heard . . .

WARD: I know. But don't worry. I think that we're clear.

GRAY: The Oracle speaks! What did you say on Sunday? We had Cromwell's word, and he was forty miles away! *(He throws away his sword.)*

WARD: They will hunt you down.

GRAY: You mean they won't here? *(he deliberately rips up his green ribbon)*

WARD: You should not do that. It is a symbol of –

GRAY: I know! The brotherhood of man. I saw that at work in Burford. Troopers from our own army hacking us down like sheep – and enjoying it.

WARD *(quietly)*: They were misled.

GRAY: *They* were misled? Ah, that is the answer! Disagree with me and you are misled. Perhaps they are right after all. Nothing will ever change. The rich will be rich for ever and the poor will be poor for ever, and the poor will betray each other for ever and ever and ever!

WARD: That is the voice of despair.

GRAY: It is the voice of experience. *My* experience.

WARD: Then I am sorry for you.

GRAY: Be sorry for yourself. *(He stands, looking without his armour a sorry sort of wretch. He hands* WARD *his flask)* You might need this. *(He walks away, turns, and speaks to* FALLON*)*

GRAY: Are you coming?

FALLON *shakes his head.*

GRAY: So. *(Raises a hand. Exits.)*

WARD: You're sure you don't want to go with him?

FALLON: Not where he's going. Are you ready?

WARD: Ready enough.

FALLON *helps* WARD *to his feet. Exit.*

Scene 3

RICHARDS' *kitchen. Wednesday.*

JOAN *is swabbing the floor. In acute contrast to her previous immaculate appearance she is dirty and bedraggled. The* HOUSEKEEPER *is sitting at the table drinking ale and gnawing at a huge piece of beef.*

The clock chimes twelve. From outside we hear PYKE's *voice.*

PYKE: Right, get your vittles and be back here sharp.

The HOUSEKEEPER *hurriedly gets up and hides the beef.* PYKE *enters.*

PYKE: What's for dinner?

HOUSEKEEPER: Pease pudding.

PYKE *(sourly)*: Master had beef.

HOUSEKEEPER: Aye, and he ate it all up.

PYKE *pours out ale as the* HOUSEKEEPER *ladles out an unsavoury mess.*

PYKE *(stares at his bowl)* : A man deserves something better than this.

The Sea Green Man

HOUSEKEEPER: Eat it and be grateful. If them mutineers had got their way you wouldn't be eating anything.

PYKE grunts and begins eating.

HOUSEKEEPER: What's happening to them, anyway?
PYKE: Who?
HOUSEKEEPER: The mutineerers. Them Levelling men.
PYKE: They're locked up in church. *(with relish)* They're going to shoot them tomorrow.

JOAN raises her head.

HOUSEKEEPER *(shocked)*: What, all of them?
PYKE: All four hundred, 'cepting them that got killed on Sunday and them that got away. They're still rounding men up in the woods. I saw one brought in just this morning. They'd given him a whacking.
HOUSEKEEPER *(whispers)*: Four hundred.

Throughout the following exchange JOAN slowly creeps towards PYKE and the HOUSEKEEPER.

PYKE: That's right, and they deserve it. The whole boiling of them stirring up trouble and all. *(He pushes his bowl away.)*
PYKE: Is there an apple or something?
HOUSEKEEPER *(relenting a little)*: You can have some damson jam. Get a spoon from the drawer.

She goes for the jam. PYKE opens the drawer. JOAN is very aware of PYKE's next action.

PYKE: What's this? *(takes out a pistol)* Master must have left it here on Sunday night. You'd better see he gets it. *(He attacks the jam.)* I'm going to see them tomorrow.
HOUSEKEEPER: Who?
PYKE *(irritably)*: Them green men. I'm going to see them shot. *(ruminatively)* I've not seen anyone killed since they hanged that blind man and his son. Stole a horse they did. But I've never

seen a shooting. And four hundred, that'll be something to see that will.

HOUSEKEEPER: But four hundred . . .

PYKE: They're traitors ain't they? They don't believe in nothing, they don't, not marriage or nothing.

HOUSEKEEPER *(truly shocked)*: Never!

PYKE: That's right. And the Pope pays them.

HOUSEKEEPER: The Pope!

PYKE: Yes. He sends priests over with money. All disguised they are. Dressed up like you and me. Some of them are dressed up like women!

HOUSEKEEPER: I never! *(Looks around uncomfortably as if a demonic priest is about to pop up in the kitchen.)* Makes you all queer that does, I mean, they could be anyone.

PYKE: That's right enough.

HOUSEKEEPER *(thoughtfully)*: But I thought . . .

PYKE: Thought what?

HOUSEKEEPER: I thought that they were against him . . . the Pope.

PYKE: What do you know about it?

HOUSEKEEPER: Only what you tell me, Mr Pyke. But what about Tyler?

PYKE: He's in the lock-up.

HOUSEKEEPER: He should have been whipped from the town long since. He started to teach the children to read!

PYKE: He'll get worse than a whipping this time. *(He notices* JOAN.*)* What are you gawping at?

HOUSEKEEPER: Are you idling?

JOAN *stares at her with unconcealed defiance.*

HOUSEKEEPER: Ah, Miss Impudence, there's a cure for you. *(She swipes* JOAN *with a filthy cloth.)* Get back to your work. Get back!

During this exchange PYKE *has slouched to the door.*

PYKE: Do you want to come? Tomorrow?

HOUSEKEEPER *(with hideous coyness)*: I might, if you asks me nice.

PYKE: I'll see. *(Exits.)*

> The HOUSEKEEPER *runs to the cupboard and takes out the beef and gnaws it greedily as* JOAN *bends to her toil.*

Scene 4

A country scene.

> WARD *and* FALLON. *Both are without armour but still wear their green ribbons.* WARD, *clearly unable to go further, collapses.* FALLON *offers him his flask but this is empty.*

FALLON: We've lost, haven't we?

WARD *(a painful, racking cough)*: This time. We lost a battle but the war goes on.

FALLON *(unconvinced and looking around nervously)*: Yes?

WARD: Yes.

FALLON *(bleakly)*: It's over.

WARD: Don't say that, Brother.

FALLON: It's true though, isn't it? *(Tries clumsily to make* WARD *more comfortable.)* What went wrong?

WARD *(shakes his head)*: Don't say wrong.

FALLON: That won't do. It won't do! We are finished and done with.

WARD: The world will hear of us.

FALLON: Aye? Gray heard us, didn't he? And he ran. The whole army heard us – and what has happened?

WARD: They didn't understand.

FALLON *(passionately)*: You said that to Gray, but what's the use of keeping on saying it? We told them and told them, and what has happened? Maybe Gray spoke the truth; we are wrong and they are right.

WARD: No!

FALLON: How can you be so sure? Those, the other troopers, they have minds of their own, too. Are we to put our minds above theirs?

WARD: Yes.

FALLON: You will never give in, will you?

WARD: No.

FALLON: They'll kill you for it.

WARD: All the King's army could not do that, and they tried hard enough for three years. *(coughs painfully)* I owe Christ a life.

FALLON: Corporal, I fought for three years as well.

WARD: Did you fight for a lie?

FALLON: No! I fought for the truth as I saw it, and I would fight for another three years – even for a half-truth. I would! I would walk every bloody footprint of those miles again to hold what we have gained. And we did get something. We did! We killed a king, and that was no mean thing to do. Every tyrant who ever lives will shake in his bed forever more; but . . .

WARD: But . . .?

FALLON *(passionately)*: But I will not be put up against a wall in some petty town and be shot for it. That is no end for me.

WARD: Do you think that you will live for ever? No. I should not have said that. Forgive me. *(FALLON visibly does.)* I understand.

FALLON: I wish I did.

Faint sounds of cavalry, shots, shouts, the sound of dogs baying. FALLON *flinches.*

WARD: They are on our heels. Go, Brother. Try to get to Northampton. We have friends there. Go!

FALLON *(torn between loyalty and fear)*: You're sure?

WARD: Sure.

FALLON *hesitates, then takes off his green ribbon, folds it, and carefully puts it in his pocket.* WARD *nods approval.* FALLON *throws away his sword.*

WARD: It is unstained.

FALLON *(kneels, takes WARD's hand)*: God with you.

WARD: God with you, Brother.
FALLON: I –

The sound of the pursuers grows nearer.

WARD: Go!
FALLON *(moving away)*: Corporal –

Whoops and halloos from the pursuers.

WARD: Run! Keep the faith – and tell the story.

FALLON *exits. Cries of the pursuers etc.* ROUNDHEADS *charge on stage. They seize* WARD *brutally.*

ROUNDHEAD: Got you! Captain! Here's another! Captain!

A CAPTAIN *enters.*

CAPTAIN: Well, well. Another dog. *(He pokes* WARD *with his sword, hacking at his green ribbon.)* And all dressed up like a maypole. We'll do a dance with him! Up! Up! On your feet, dog.

WARD *painfully tries to rise but collapses.*

CAPTAIN *(turning* WARD *over with his foot)*: He'll last for the firing squad. Take him.

ROUNDHEADS *exit dragging* WARD *by the heels.*

Scene 5

Wednesday afternoon.
The lock-up. A bare room with a cot. A barred door. TYLER *is sitting on the cot singing.*

TYLER: 'Pray that Jerusalem may have, peace and prosperity' –

STOCKS *appears at the door.*

STOCKS *(almost apologetically)*: You shouldn't be singing.

TYLER: Is it a crime now to sing a psalm? That song we sang when we broke the ranks of Belial at Naseby.

STOCKS: Belial?

TYLER: King Charles. I wore that uniform then. *(points at* STOCKS*)*

STOCKS *(impressed)*: You fought at Naseby?

TYLER: I carried a pike on that field.

STOCKS *(shakes his head)*: And now you're in here.

TYLER: 'Though I walk through the valley of the shadow of death I shall fear no evil.'

STOCKS: Aye? Lucky for you. Aren't you worried about that girl of yours?

TYLER: Do you have a child?

STOCKS *(ruefully)*: I've got five.

TYLER: Then you will know how a father feels. But God who sees the sparrow fall will watch over her.

STOCKS: You really do believe it, don't you?

TYLER: God is with me. How can I not believe. I tell you –

Outside a bellow of Shun! *The crash of arms being presented.* STOCKS *raises his finger to his lips in a warning gesture. Goes to his desk, and stands to attention as* HASLAM *enters.*

STOCKS: Sir!

HASLAM: All in order, Stocks?

STOCKS: Yes, Sir.

HASLAM: How is the prisoner?

STOCKS: No trouble, Sir. *(His voice indicates that although* TYLER *is no physical problem he is troubling* STOCKS.*)*

HASLAM *(alert to this)*: Have you been talking to the prisoner?

STOCKS *(stiffly)*: Only in the line of duty, Sir.

HASLAM: You know who he is, don't you.

STOCKS: Civilian prisoner, Sir. John Tyler.

HASLAM: Yes, but he is no common prisoner.

STOCKS: Sir?

HASLAM: He is more dangerous than a thief or a burglar. Much more dangerous.

STOCKS: Sir?

HASLAM: Men such as *he* plunder men's minds.

TYLER *begins singing another psalm*.

TYLER: 'By the waters of Babylon, where we sat down. Yea, we wept when we remembered Zion.' *(continues singing)*

HASLAM: He is singing.

STOCKS: A psalm, Sir, from the Holy Book.

HASLAM: Open the cell.

STOCKS: Yes, Sir.

Inside the cell. STOCKS, *a loyal trooper, stands by the door but listens intently to what follows.*

TYLER *(Looks up defiantly as* HASLAM *enters. Quotes)*: 'O daughter of Babylon which art to be destroyed. Happy shall he be that rewardeth thee as thou has served us!' Yes, happy.

HASLAM *(sits, pacifying)*: Mr Tyler –

TYLER *(exaggerated surprise)*: Mister!

HASLAM: Yes, *Mister*. What can I say to you?

TYLER: What can I say to you?

HASLAM *(courteously)*: May I speak to you?

TYLER: As you spoke to me in my house when you took me without a warrant? And as you spoke to me when you gave my daughter into the hand of my enemy?

HASLAM: I was merely obeying orders.

TYLER: Aye, a dog obeys its master's orders. Are you a mere dog to bark and bite when the whistle sounds? And are we silly sheep to bleat and baah when you bite?

HASLAM *(sharply)*: That's enough. I would not let Master Richards use such language to you.

TYLER: Yes, you refuse to bark but you are ready to bite, or why am I here?

HASLAM *(swallowing this)*: Mister Tyler, it gives me no pleasure to see you here, but we must all be moderate –

TYLER: Moderate! Were we moderate when we executed the King? *(laughs)* I know your moderation; kneel down when the master passes and that is moderate. Stand up and that is rebellion.

HASLAM: You preach, do you not?

TYLER: I do.

HASLAM: Could you do that before the war? *(STOCKS nods, taking the point.)* Indeed you know that you could not. You would have been whipped for it. Is that not tolerance of belief? Is it not?

TYLER: When I speak of the Kingdom of Heaven I am let free to preach, but when I preach of Heaven upon Earth – why . . . *(points to his battered face.)*

HASLAM: That is not religion it is politics.

TYLER: Aye, I may talk of anything save that which affects me.

HASLAM: Leave politics for . . . for

TYLER: For my betters, like Richards who has my daughter.

HASLAM: No harm will come to her, I promise you that. My word on it. I know that you are anxious about her but we all bear wounds in this world.

TYLER: Do not talk to me of wounds. *(He opens his shirt revealing a long scar.)* I got that at Naseby. Do you know what our captain said as the King's horsemen came down upon us? He said, stand firm. Stand firm for freedom. *(Laughs. An eloquent wave of his hand.)*

HASLAM: Well, I could show you a scar or two come to that.

TYLER: Aye, but you are outside and I am inside.

HASLAM: If you would stop your agitating . . .

TYLER: Never! Never while I have breath in my body.

HASLAM *(very sharp)*: Very well, Tyler. I see that you are a fanatic. *(Looks at STOCKS who obviously agrees. TYLER laughs.)*

HASLAM: So, laugh away. *(He goes to the door. Turns and makes a last appeal to reason.)* Man, do you not see what you are up against? General Cromwell has two thousand men in this town and ten thousand more at his beck and call. Overwhelming force and the whole of England against you.

TYLER: So it was when the war began. But we won.

HASLAM *(taken aback)*: That was different.

TYLER: Was it?

HASLAM: Man, how can common people be given a vote? They would not know for what they voted.

TYLER: Then they must be taught.

HASLAM: You are insane. Would you have all men go to school to learn their ABC?

TYLER: Yes. How else can men be equal?

HASLAM: Forget equality. That story is over.

TYLER: That story will never end.

HASLAM *(a last appeal)*: I am not against you, Tyler.

TYLER *(implacably)*: Those who are not with us are against us.

HASLAM: Then you must take your punishment. *(walks out of cell, saying to STOCKS:)* What can you do with such men?

STOCKS: Not a lot, Sir.

> TYLER, *under extreme emotional pressure rushes to the cell door and shouts:*

TYLER: 'Happy shall he be that taketh and dasheth *thy* little ones against the stone!' *(bellows)* Psalm one hundred and thirty eight!

Scene 6

Wednesday evening.
> RICHARDS' *kitchen. The* HOUSEKEEPER *looming over her,* JOAN *is swabbing out some filthy jugs.*

HOUSEKEEPER: See you get them clean.

> PYKE *enters.*

PYKE: Master Coles has come, and the other gentlemen. They're at the front door.

HOUSEKEEPER: But the Master isn't back, yet.

PYKE: I can't help that, can I? Anyway, they're here so you'd better attend to them.

> HOUSEKEEPER *exits grumbling.*

HOUSEKEEPER: Why can't folk stay at home . . .

PYKE pours out a jug of ale and sits down. Looks at JOAN.

PYKE: Not Miss Prim now, are you? Where's your preaching now? What's the matter, been struck dumb, have you? *(JOAN remains silent.)* Looking forward to tomorrow I am. Be all day, they will, shooting the mutineerers. I'd join the shooters, I would –

FRANCIS enters. PYKE hastily stands up, whips off his hat.

PYKE *(grovelling)*: Evening, Master. I was just saying your father ain't back yet. Master Coles is here –
FRANCIS: I know that.
PYKE: Ah, well. *(He gives a longing look at the ale.)* I'll get along then, Sir. *(Slouches out.)*

FRANCIS sits on the table swinging his legs and munching an apple while watching JOAN.

FRANCIS: You're dirty.
JOAN: The dirt is from your house.
FRANCIS *(shrilly indignant)*: Our house isn't dirty!

JOAN does not deign to answer but holds up her filthy dishcloth.

FRANCIS *(inspired)*: They're old pots. They're for the dogs. The dogs eat out of them. *(Another inspiration.)* And now a cat is cleaning them. A dirty cat.

JOAN does not bother to answer but gives FRANCIS a disdainful look.

FRANCIS *(searching for another taunt)*: Your father is dirty, too. He is a dirty nasty common worker. Now he's in the lock-up because he is a thief.
JOAN *(stung)*: Your father is the thief.
FRANCIS: He isn't! He isn't! Don't dare say that.

JOAN *(striking back)*:
> The law pursues the man or woman
> Who steals the goose from off the common,
> But lets the greater villain loose,
> Who steals the common from the goose.

That's your father. He stole the commons.

FRANCIS: Liar!

> *He throws the apple at* JOAN *who laughs contemptuously as it misses her by metres.*
>
> *A clatter of horses in the yard.* RICHARDS *enters, hugely self-satisfied. Shouts to* PYKE *off stage.*

RICHARDS: Yes, I'll be with them in one minute.

> FRANCIS *runs to* RICHARDS *who ruffles his hair fondly.*

RICHARDS: Ah, child! Do you know where your father has been? Hey? He has been to Burford Manor House, and do you know who he met there? Why, he met Oliver Cromwell! Do you know who he is?

FRANCIS *(with ghastly piety)*: I know that he is a great man, Father.

RICHARDS: He is! He is! He is a general of the army!

FRANCIS *(simulating awe)*: A General!

RICHARDS: One of the greatest in the land. His sword struck down our enemies and now his voice is mighty. And he is angry, Francis.

FRANCIS: Angry, Father?

RICHARDS: Yes, he sees the wickedness of the mutineers and he is minded to shoot them all!

JOAN: And what of my father?

> RICHARDS *looks pompously at* JOAN *but is clearly not so cruel as to suggest that* TYLER *is to be shot too.*

RICHARDS: When your father –

> FRANCIS, *knowing perfectly well what his father is about to say, maliciously butts in.*

FRANCIS: She says that we are dirty, Father. And she said that you are a thief.
RICHARDS: What?
FRANCIS: She says you stole our land.
RICHARDS: Dare you say so?
JOAN: He called my father a thief.
FRANCIS: I did not.
JOAN: Indeed you know that you did.
FRANCIS *(anxious to divert attention)*: She threw that apple at me.
RICHARDS: Pick it up.
JOAN: He threw it, let him pick it up.
RICHARDS *(exasperated)*: Do you do nothing but argue! Pick it up I say.

JOAN *stubbornly shakes her head.*

RICHARDS: You will not eat until you do.
JOAN: Then I shall never eat! And what of my father? What is to happen to him?
RICHARDS: What should happen to the father of such a child!

The HOUSEKEEPER *enters.*

HOUSEKEEPER: Master, the gentlemen are waiting.
RICHARDS: I'm coming. No food for her while that apple lies there.

Exits followed by FRANCIS *who sticks out his tongue at* JOAN.

HOUSEKEEPER: Your father is in for a shock, hussy – yes, and you are, too. The day isn't over yet. *(Exits.)*

Scene 7

The passage of an hour or so. JOAN *kneeling. Half asleep. The door opens and the* HOUSEKEEPER *enters. Through the door we can hear a semi-drunken revelry. Shouts of:* Shoot them all! Hang them! Flog them!

HOUSEKEEPER: Are you sleeping brat? Get on with your work.

She unlocks a cupboard and takes out bottles of wine, as JOAN *wearily swabs a jug.*

RICHARDS *(off-stage)*: Mistress Pratt!
HOUSEKEEPER: Coming, Sir.
RICHARDS *(booming)*: We'll finish with Tyler.

A bay of approbation from the other men: Him especially! That dog. *etc.*

HOUSEKEEPER: You hear that? Your father is going to get what he deserves.
RICHARDS: Pratt!

HOUSEKEEPER *exits.* JOAN, *thoroughly alarmed, runs to the door and listens for a moment, hesitates, then grabs a basket and a cloth. Reaches up to a shelf and takes down her Bible, hesitates again then resolutely takes the pistol from the drawer, puts it into her basket and tip-toes to the door. As she reaches the door* FRANCIS *enters.*

FRANCIS *(suspiciously)*: Where are you going?
JOAN: Mind your own business.

FRANCIS *runs in front of* JOAN *and blocks her way.*

FRANCIS: I said where are you going? If you don't tell me I'll shout for Papa.
JOAN *(hesitates, then recovers her wits)*: I'm going to the vegetable garden – for peas.
FRANCIS: There aren't any peas. They're not out yet.
JOAN: No. I meant comfrey, for a salad.
FRANCIS *(accusingly)*: You said peas.
JOAN: I meant comfrey.
FRANCIS: Why are you going out now? It's almost dark. I know! You're trying to run away!
JOAN: No I'm not.
FRANCIS: Yes you are. I know you are!

JOAN: All right. Listen, I'll tell you something.

FRANCIS: What?

JOAN: It's a secret. *(She looms over FRANCIS.)* A secret. You mustn't tell anyone.

FRANCIS: I won't.

JOAN: Promise.

FRANCIS: I promise, I promise.

JOAN: You know the pie you had at supper?

FRANCIS: Yes?

JOAN: Well . . . cross your heart and hope to die?

FRANCIS: Yes, yes.

JOAN: The pie with all the jam in it?

FRANCIS *(snuffling with greed)*: Yes!

JOAN: It wasn't all eaten! There's some left.

FRANCIS: Where?

JOAN: I hid it. And listen, if I can have a bit, you can have the rest.

FRANCIS *hesitates*.

JOAN: Jam . . .

FRANCIS: All right – but I have most.

JOAN *(affecting sullenness)*: That's not fair.

FRANCIS: You shouldn't have any at all!

JOAN: Oh . . . all right, you have most.

FRANCIS: Where is it?

JOAN: In the cellar.

FRANCIS *(alarmed)*: The cellar?

JOAN: Yes, come on.

FRANCIS *hesitates*.

JOAN: It's only on the top step. Come on.

She crosses the kitchen to the cellar door and opens it. FRANCIS peers nervously into the blackness.

FRANCIS: I can't see anything.

JOAN: No, but you can see this! *(She gives FRANCIS a resounding box on the ear.)* Take that!

She pushes FRANCIS *into the cellar, slams the door on him, and rushes out.*

Scene 8

Wednesday night.

The lock-up. TYLER *is sitting on the cot. He lifts his head as he hears the clatter of horses.*

VOICE *(off-stage)*: Stocks!

STOCKS: Sir!

VOICE: A prisoner. Hold him overnight. We'll stick him in the church tomorrow. *(harshly)* Come on, you.

The cell door is opened and WARD, *manacled, is bundled through. He sprawls to the floor.* TYLER *goes to his assistance.*

VOICE: Sign for him.

TYLER *attends to* WARD.

VOICE: Right. We'll pick him up tomorrow.

Sound of a door slamming. Horses moving away.

TYLER: Guard!

STOCKS *appears at the cell door.*

TYLER: Let me have a cloth and some water.

STOCKS: Well . . . if there aren't any officers about. *(Exits.)*

TYLER: Come on, Brother.

He helps WARD, *loosens collar etc. and helps him onto the cot.* STOCKS *peers through the cell door, unlocks it and passes through a jug, some cloth, and a flask.*

STOCKS: There's some wine.

TYLER: Thank you. It won't be forgotten.

STOCKS *(ruefully)*: I don't want it remembered.

TYLER *pours some wine in* WARD*'s mouth.* WARD *revives.*

WARD: Who are you, Samaritan?

TYLER *(staunching* WARD*'s wound)*: John Tyler. Cobbler. Of Burford. And you?

WARD: Ward. Corporal of horse. Reynold's Regiment. What are you doing in here?

TYLER: Locked up while the trouble is on.

WARD *looks at him shrewdly.*

TYLER *(understanding the look)*: I'm no informer.

WARD *(gives* TYLER *a hard stare then nods, satisfied)*: You've been knocked about a bit. The troopers do it?

TYLER: No.

WARD: Where did you get that, then? *(Motioning to* TYLER*'s face.)*

TYLER: Preaching.

WARD *(guffaws at the irony, then groans)*: Don't know why I'm laughing. *(He takes a little more wine.)* Not popular, hey?

TYLER: Levellers aren't round here.

WARD: You a Leveller? *(nods approval)* What's happened?

TYLER: Don't you know?

WARD: I've been on the run for three days.

TYLER: Well, your guess is as good as mine. I've been locked up in here since Monday morning. But I heard them *(jerks thumb to the cell door)* say that your lads are locked in the church.

WARD: The church, hey? They know how to pick the right places.

TYLER *(delicately, not wishing to appear to pry)*: What was it about, the mutiny?

WARD *(looks speculatively at* TYLER*)*: You know about the Catholic rebellion in Ireland? *(*TYLER *nods.)* And you know Parliament wants to send the Army over to crush it?

STOCKS *(appears at the cell door)*: You shouldn't be talking in there.

TYLER: No talking, no singing!

WARD: Where's the harm? You can hear us.

STOCKS: All right. But keep your voices down. *(He stays at the cell door.)*

WARD: Well . . . Parliament. They say that they are frightened the Irish will invade England and bring back the King and Popery.

STOCKS: Suppose they did?

WARD: Man, how could they? We command the seas and if they did land, every man in England would be against them. They would be slaughtered as they stepped on shore.

STOCKS: Then why should Parliament want to send the Army?

WARD: To grab land. Why else?

TYLER: That's the tale!

WARD: Well, whatever the reason, the Generals chose regiments to go to Ireland. Picked the names out of a hat!

TYLER: And you refused to go.

WARD: I did, and many like me. I joined the Army to make Englishmen free, not to enslave Irishmen. Why should I put men and women to the sword because they want for themselves what I want for myself?

STOCKS: No man had to go against his wishes. He could leave the Army. General Cromwell said so himself.

WARD: Why should we leave the Army?

STOCKS *(taken aback)*: Well . . . if you won't obey orders . . .

WARD: Whose orders? We asked for a General Council of the Army, every regiment sending its elected agitator. Was that not our right?

STOCKS: Well . . .

WARD: You know it was. Were not the terms written down in the Agreement of the People? I was at the debate in Putney church and I saw it written down; 'No man shall be constrained to serve in any war.' What makes us different from other armies but that? We wear a uniform but we are still free men. Aye, not paid butchers like the Spanish or the French but God's Englishmen! Soldiers of Christ Jesus! That message I heard in the wind at Edge Hill right when the cavalleros were hacking us down.

A long pause.

TYLER: You were at the Putney debates?

WARD: That I was. I saw Cromwell there, and Ireton, all the Grandees as they have now become. We made a covenant with them but they kept not their covenant with us. *(with passion)* They kept it not!

TYLER: You were an agitator?

WARD *(proudly)*: I was – am! Elected by my troop.

STOCKS: They'll agitate you tomorrow. *(A shocked silence.)* Sorry, I shouldn't have said that.

WARD: Said what? What do you mean?

STOCKS: Nothing.

WARD: Speak plainly, man.

TYLER: Speak out.

WARD: Do you think I cannot look the truth in the face?

A long pause.

STOCKS: They are bringing out the firing squad tomorrow.

Scene 9

Thursday night.

JOAN *is hurrying through a wood. A general air of menace. Dogs barking in the distance etc. From the darkness a figure looms.* JOAN *gives a little scream. It is* GROTE, *who grabs her.*

GROTE: You! What are you doing here?

JOAN *(not afraid)*: None of your business.

GROTE: You ought to be at Master Richards'. Maybe I'd better take you back.

JOAN: You just try! *(on the attack)* What are you doing here?

GROTE: Never you mind.

JOAN: Poaching?

GROTE: I said never you mind. What you got in there?

JOAN *(double bluffing)*: A pistol!

GROTE: Impudence!

He draws near in ghastly, Groteish fashion. JOAN *stands her ground and pushes him off.*

JOAN: Get away from me! I said get away. You smell!
GROTE: What! *(Raises his hand threateningly.)*
JOAN: You'd better not!
GROTE: Don't think I couldn't.

JOAN jerks her head contemptuously and moves away. GROTE *steps in front of her.*

GROTE: I want to know what you've got in that there basket.
JOAN *(anxious to get away)*: A Bible. *(Takes it out.)*
GROTE: What you carrying that about for?
JOAN: It's for my father.
GROTE: He's in the lock-up.
JOAN: I know that. Richards said I could take it to him.
GROTE: Oh. *(He snatches the Bible and paws it.)*
JOAN: Give it back. I said give it to me. *(Takes the Bible.)* You can't read anyway.
GROTE: What's the good of reading? It don't put bacon in your belly.
JOAN: It feeds your mind.
GROTE *(puzzled)*: You can read, can't you?
JOAN: Of course I can. *(She tries to edge around* GROTE.*)*
GROTE: 'Tain't natural, women reading.

JOAN moves away a step or so.

GROTE: Women should be in the house, see, doing the cooking and all that. *(ruminatively)* When they bain't be in the fields working.
JOAN: Yes, while you're in the ale house.
GROTE: What's wrong with that? A man's got to have his fun. 'Sides, women be lower than men, everyone knows that.
JOAN *(still moving away; contemptuously)*: Do they?
GROTE: Parson says so.

JOAN: He would.

GROTE *(grumbling to himself)*: Women, they be preaching and agitating all over the place.

JOAN: Yes, and one day they will agitate in Parliament.

GROTE: Parliament! That's Levelling talk.

JOAN: Yes. Levelling.

GROTE: Shouldn't be allowed. Pulling everything down.

JOAN: Levelling means bringing up as well as knocking down. Everyone equal. No more bondsmen. No more slaves.

GROTE: There ain't any slaves in England.

JOAN: Women are slaves. You're wife is, anyway. You're a slave, too, but you don't know it.

GROTE *(turning savage again)*: You watch your mouth.

> JOAN *has a sudden idea. Stops dead.*

JOAN: What's that?

GROTE *(alarmed)*: What's what?

JOAN *(artfully taking a step or two backwards and lowering her voice)*: A man. Over there.

GROTE: Where?

JOAN: He's gone behind that tree. It's Richards' gamekeeper.

GROTE *(terrorstruck)*: A keeper!

> GROTE *takes to his heels.* JOAN *hurries on.*

Scene 10

The same night. The lock-up. This should show the ante-chamber, as it were. A table, a chair and a lantern.

> STOCKS *is standing against the cell door blocking the view from the lock-up proper.*

> JOAN *enters.* STOCKS, *not recognising the bedraggled girl, is peremptory.*

STOCKS: Hoi! What do you want?

JOAN: May I see my father? He is here, isn't he?

STOCKS: That depends on who he is.

JOAN: John Tyler.

STOCKS *(moves from the door and peers at JOAN, amazed)*: Are you . . . are you his daughter? What has happened to you?

JOAN *(dryly)*: I was put to work.

STOCKS: Why, this is not right.

TYLER *(appears at the cell door)*: Joan!

STOCKS: Get back! Back I tell you!

TYLER *retreats.*

STOCKS *(looks at JOAN and shakes his head)*: What do you want?

JOAN: To speak to my father. Just to talk to him for a moment.

STOCKS, *deeply moved by JOAN's state, disobeys orders.*

STOCKS: You're not allowed to but – go on. Hurry up.

JOAN *(at the cell door)*: Father.

TYLER *(appears at the door)*: Joan, child! What's happened to you?

JOAN *(urgently)*: It's all right, father. *(drops her voice)* I have something for you.

STOCKS: Speak up!

JOAN: I have a Bible for you.

TYLER: Ah! That will be a grace and a comfort.

JOAN *cautiously puts her hand in her basket.*

STOCKS: What are you doing there?

JOAN: A Bible. May I give my father a Bible?

STOCKS: No, you may not. You shouldn't even be speaking to the prisoner.

JOAN: Just a Bible. *(She holds it up.)*

TYLER: Would you deny us the word of God *(significantly)* on this of all nights?

STOCKS *(weakens a little)*: Well . . .

WARD *(out of sight in the cell but his voice carrying authority)*: Let him have it!

STOCKS *(surrendering)*: I would deny no man the word of the Lord.

Act Two

STOCKS *takes the keys and begins to fiddle with the lock. This should be a protracted piece of business as* STOCKS *curses and* JOAN *is on tip-toe with anxiety.*

STOCKS: Blast it, the key is jammed. *(He tries again.)* Got it!

As the key turns and JOAN's *eyes light up, there is a shout of* Guard! STOCKS *stiffens to attention as* HASLAM *enters, very much the stiff subaltern inspecting the Guard.*

HASLAM: What the Dev – what is this girl doing here, trooper? *(His voice and manner suggest that he suspects* STOCKS *of immoral conduct.)*

STOCKS *(aware of this, answers stiffly)*: The prisoner's daughter, Sir. Tyler. She's brought him a Bible.

HASLAM: A Bible? Give it to me.

JOAN *(swallows her pride, curtsies as she hands over the Bible)* Sir.

HASLAM takes the Bible and flicks through it.

HASLAM: Very well. He may have this. But you, out and try having a wash.

JOAN: But –

HASLAM: No buts. Out.

As JOAN *does not move he takes her by the shoulder.* JOAN, *desperate, tries to resist.*

HASLAM: Out!

His patience tried, he pushes her to the door. JOAN *stumbles, basket swings, and the pistol falls onto the floor. There is a shocked silence.* HASLAM *bends and picks up the pistol and looks grimly at* JOAN.

TYLER: Oh, daughter! What have you done to us!

Scene 11

Late Thursday night.

RICHARDS' *kitchen.* JOAN *is defiantly facing* RICHARDS, *the* HOUSEKEEPER *and* PYKE.

RICHARDS *(in a towering rage)*: Thief! I take you into my house and you steal from me. And a pistol! Wicked wretch. Spawn of the Devil.

JOAN: That I am not.

RICHARDS: Malignant wickedness!

JOAN *(pointing to* PYKE*)*: He said my father was to be shot.

RICHARDS: And so he should be. Shot dead!

JOAN: Was I to do nothing?

RICHARDS: Defiance, always defiance! Do you think that you can speak to your betters so?

JOAN: I have no betters.

RICHARDS *(staggered)*: Hear her! Do you hear her? She has no betters! A cobbler's daughter! A wretch in arms against lawful authority. A rebel defying those whom God has placed over you.

JOAN: You were a rebel against those God had placed over *you*. But God has placed none over me save the Sanctified.

RICHARDS: The Sanctified? Do you speak of Saints to me? You, a wicked, unruly thief?

JOAN: I am no thief.

RICHARDS: Did you not steal the pistol? You could be hanged for that. Do you hear me? Hanged!

JOAN: Then hang me.

RICHARDS: More defiance! Wickedness, dishonesty, disobedience!

JOAN: I am none of those.

RICHARDS *(bellowing)*: You are! Did you not . . . *(somewhat at a loss for words)* . . . did you not refuse to pick up that apple?

JOAN *bursts out laughing, not sardonically or ironically but with genuine childish amusement at this ludicrous remark.*

RICHARDS: She laughs! Mark that! Original sin!

> HOUSEKEEPER *and* PYKE *are suitably shocked at this theological revelation.*

HOUSEKEEPER: Original sin!
PYKE: Sin!
RICHARDS: Aye, sin. She laughs at me, mocks me in my own home. Well take her; take her and whip her. Whip the wickedness from her.
HOUSEKEEPER: That will be a pleasure.
RICHARDS: Take her into the scullery and when I hear her cry out then I will know that the Devil has left her.
JOAN: Then you will wait for ever for there is no Devil in me.
RICHARDS: Take her!

> PYKE *moves towards* JOAN *but* RICHARDS *is not prepared to have that.*

RICHARDS *(to the* HOUSEKEEPER*)*: You take her.

> JOAN *is bundled into the scullery. Various crashing noises as pots and pans are knocked down as* JOAN *does not succumb without a struggle. Cries from the* HOUSEKEEPER*; Get down! Down! etc. We hear the thwack and swish of the whipping.* RICHARDS *prowls about the kitchen as the whipping continues. There is not a murmur from* JOAN. *Finally* RICHARDS *cannot stand it any longer.*

RICHARDS: Enough! Enough!

> *Enter* JOAN *and a dishevelled* HOUSEKEEPER *who is in a worse state than* JOAN.

RICHARDS *(rather disturbed)*: Take her to the cellar. Lock her in. Don't stand gawking! Take her!

> *The* HOUSEKEEPER *takes* JOAN*'s elbow.* JOAN *disdainfully shakes her off and walks from the room followed by the* HOUSEKEEPER.

RICHARDS *(bangs the table)*: Never have I seen such stubborn wickedness in a child.

PYKE: What will you do with her, Master?

RICHARDS: I know what I would like to do.

PYKE: Send her to the House of Correction.

RICHARDS: I would like nothing better, but . . .

PYKE: But what, Sir?

RICHARDS: General Cromwell is showing mercy to the mutineers.

PYKE: Mercy!

RICHARDS: Yes, only a handful are to be shot *(Deep disappointment on* PYKE'*s face.)* He wants these troubles ended quickly so it might be as well to follow his example. Sometimes we must tread in the footprints of great men. But one thing I shall do for sure.

PYKE: Yes, Master?

RICHARDS: I will rid us of John Tyler, once and for all.

PYKE *(eagerly)*: Aye, Sir?

RICHARDS: Aye. You know Mistress Webb? *(*PYKE *nods.)* Get her.

PYKE: Now?

RICHARDS *(exasperated)*: Yes, now! Is every order I give to be questioned?

PYKE *(grovelling)*: No, Master. No, never that . . . but it's late. She'll be in bed.

RICHARDS: Then drag her from it!

PYKE: Yes, Master. *(Hurries from kitchen.)*

Scene 12

Thursday morning. A sickly dawn light. Cocks crowing etc.

JOAN is in the cellar determinedly trying to hack her way out. Ideally there should be a grille above her head. FRANCIS *appears at the grille and peers down.*

FRANCIS: Who is in the cellar now?

JOAN *stops her effort to escape.*

FRANCIS: Who is in the cellar? Who was whipped and is in the cellar?

JOAN *glances up then contemptuously ignores* FRANCIS.

FRANCIS: The cat is in the cellar. The cat is in the cellar with the dirty nasty spiders. *(Waits for a reaction which does not come.)* The cat is in the cellar. You're going to be kept there for ever and ever and then you'll be hanged for stealing.

JOAN: Then I can't be kept here for ever, can I?

FRANCIS: Oh, clever cat. Cat. Cat. *(Seeks for a devastating attack.)* The rats come out in there at night. Great big rats.

JOAN: Your home is full of them. I saw them in your bedroom.

FRANCIS *(terrified)*: You didn't! You didn't! That's a lie. There aren't any rats in my bedroom.

JOAN: What do you know, you can't even read.

FRANCIS: I can! I can read!

JOAN: You can't even read toy books.

FRANCIS: I can!

JOAN: All right. Say the ABC.

FRANCIS: I don't want to.

JOAN: Because you can't. Your father can hardly read.

FRANCIS: He can! He's a rich man, not like your father. He's just a dirty old cobbler.

Tired of the slanging match JOAN *turns away.*

FRANCIS: All right, cat. Cat! I'll tell you a secret. Cat! A secret. My father said I shouldn't tell you but I will. Cat, your father is dead!

JOAN *looks up, horrified.*

FRANCIS *(crowing with delight)*: Yes! He's dead. Cromwell shot him last night because you stole the pistol.

JOAN: Liar! Liar!

She claws at the grille. FRANCIS *is frightened but shouts triumphantly.*

FRANCIS: It's true! True!

FRANCIS runs away. Left to herself JOAN finally breaks down and weeps.

Scene 13

Thursday. Later that morning.
TYLER's house. The GROTES are in the room, fingering tools and books.

MRS GROTE *(looking at a chair)*: That'll do us nicely.
GROTE: Ar, and these. *(Indicating tools.)* What about the books?
MRS GROTE *(contemptuously)*: We don't want them. Hold on though, they'll do for making the fire. And –

She jumps as the door opens and TYLER enters. TYLER glares at the GROTES who are the picture of guilt.

MRS GROTE: You made me jump.
TYLER: What are you two doing here?
GROTE *(nervous whine)*: Just minding the house for you. Just minding it, like.
MRS GROTE *(recovered a little, now accusatory and indignant)*: They've let you out then!
TYLER: Of course they've set me free. There was no charge against me. Where is Joan?
GROTE: Still with Master Richards, I reckon.

TYLER rummages in a corner and gets a club. The GROTES back away.

MRS GROTE: What you going to do with that?

TYLER raises the club as if about to beat the GROTES, and not averse to doing so. The GROTES cower with nervous squeals.

TYLER: I'm going to get my daughter, what do you think?

He opens the door and starts back as MRS WEBB stands there.

Act Two

TYLER: Mistress Webb!

> MRS WEBB *enters, clearly nervous and ill at ease.*

TYLER: I hope you haven't come for the rent.

MRS WEBB: No, no. *(She looks over* TYLER's *shoulder at the* GROTES.*)*

TYLER *(turns to* GROTES*)*: Get out. Out!

> *He flourishes his club and the* GROTES *hastily retreat but remain peering through the back door.*

TYLER: I'm in a hurry, Mrs Webb.

MRS WEBB: Yes, but . . . *(She lays some money on the table.)*

TYLER: What's this?

MRS WEBB: That's the rent you've paid – for the last quarter.

TYLER: I don't understand you.

MRS WEBB *(embarrassment making her sharp)*: You have to leave.

TYLER *(incredulous)*: Leave! This house?

MRS WEBB: Yes. Today. Now.

TYLER: I can't believe you – I've been a good tenant to you – ah! Is Richards behind this?

MRS WEBB: Mr Tyler, I'm sorry, truly I am, but Richards sent for me last night. He's a big man here, you know that, and I owe him money. He's got mortgages on my land. I can't afford to make an enemy of him.

TYLER: So I'm to be driven from my home.

MRS WEBB: From the town.

TYLER: And where am I to go?

MRS WEBB *(shakes her head sadly)*: That I can't say. But you have some money and I'll lend you a cart for your goods . . .

TYLER: Richards! *(Raises his club and starts for the door.)*

MRS WEBB *(alarmed)*: Mr Tyler!

> TYLER *ignores her but as he gets to the door it opens and* JOAN *enters.*

JOAN: Father!

She runs to TYLER *who drops his stick and takes her by the arms, then holds her away. The tension of the past few days and the eviction telling on him, he explodes with anger.*

TYLER: Joan, Joan. Why did you do it? You almost put a rope around my neck.

JOAN *(voice quivering)*: Father . . .

TYLER: And you – do you know what could have happened to you? We could both have been hanged!

JOAN bursts into tears. Seeing the state JOAN is in MRS WEBB cuts in.

MRS WEBB: Mr Tyler, the poor child.

TYLER: What? *(comprehends)* Yes. Yes. There chuck, there. *(He embraces JOAN.)*

JOAN *(sobbing)*: They said that you were shot dead.

TYLER *(enraged)*: Who said? Who?

JOAN: Francis.

MRS WEBB: Wickedness.

TYLER: Now, now, chuck, dry your tears.

JOAN: I'm sorry, Father, I didn't know what to do . . .

TYLER: No, I'm sorry. *(He looks at her intently.)* Are you all right?

JOAN choking back her sobs, nods.

TYLER: You were not . . . not ill treated?

JOAN *(hesitates, then, wisely, shakes her head)*: No.

TYLER: That is as well for Richards. *(He notices the GROTES at the door.)* Do you see her? Do you?

GROTE: I see neighbour.

TYLER *(explodes with rage)*: Neighbour! You dare use that word? You would not give her shelter and you call yourself that?

GROTE *(surly)*: She was with a gentleman.

TYLER *(utterly disgusted)*: Look at her. Look. See what a gentleman has done.

MRS GROTE: She's a bit dirty but that's not our fault is it? It's you going about preach –

Act Two

TYLER: Get away from this house – *(He slams the door in their faces. With a huge effort he controls himself.)* Wash and change, Joan.

MRS WEBB: Come child. I'll help you.

> JOAN *exits but* MRS WEBB *halts and turns to* TYLER.

MRS WEBB: It's a wicked shame, Mister Tyler, but take my advice. Don't go near Master Richards. He's armed and . . .

TYLER: And what?

MRS WEBB: They're going to shoot those poor soldiers today. They chose them by lot, three of them. An officer and two corporals.

TYLER *(obviously remembering* WARD*)*: Corporals?

MRS WEBB: Yes, in the church yard. Make any trouble and you could join them.

> *Exits as* TYLER *sits at the table his head in his hands.*

Scene 14

Later on Thursday.

> *Outside* TYLER'*s house. A cart laden with his possessions. The* GROTES *and other neighbours watching.* TYLER *brings out a last item and puts it on the cart. He looks around challengingly then, with* JOAN, *tries to shove the cart. It barely moves and there are malicious, stupid guffaws from the* CROWD.

VOICE: You ain't a good horse.

> *Laughter. Rude farting noises.*

TYLER *(menacingly)*: Who said that?

> *The* CROWD *fall silent.* KEMP *steps forward, disgusted.*

KEMP: I'll give you a hand.

TYLER: Bless you for that, Friend.

> *They slowly move off.*

GROTE: Good riddance – *neighbour.*

69

Scene 15

Thursday. Later. Approaching dusk.

TYLER, JOAN, *and* KEMP *pushing the cart. They are obviously having difficulty. Ideally a wheel gives way, objects fall off the cart. The spectacle should be piteously wretched.*

JOAN: Oh, Father.

TYLER *looks away as if the disaster had nothing to do with him.*

KEMP *(ruefully)*: Ah well, it never rains but it pours. *(Trying to cheer up* JOAN.*)* We'll get it put right, Missie. You'd better give us a hand here, Mister.

TYLER *slowly comes out of his slightly mad reverie.*

KEMP *(his patience tried)*: We'll have to take some stuff off. Come on. *(He starts unloading cart.)* Missie, there's a chair. *(Points off-stage.)*

JOAN *(trying to be cheerful)*: I'll get it. *(Exits.)*

KEMP *(looks after her admiringly)*: One of these days a man is going to be lucky.

TYLER *(stares fixedly at* KEMP*)*: Man?

KEMP *(uncomfortable under the stare)*: You know, your daughter. She'll make a fine wife.

TYLER: Wife? Joan a wife?

KEMP *(gruff)*: Nothing wrong in that, Mr Tyler. Getting married. It's only natural.

TYLER: Wedlock!

KEMP *(mildly reproving)*: Don't say it like that. You had a wife yourself once.

TYLER *(to himself)*: My Jenny! *(Looks at the sky and slips easily and glibly into cant.)* Now in Zion. In glory among the cherubim and seraphim, chanting endless hosannas with angels and archangels. Praises be to the Lord of Hosts . . .

KEMP *(busy working on the wheel)*: Oh, Heaven.

TYLER *(in the same visionary vein, ranting as* KEMP *works)*: Aye,

Jerusalem! Jerusalem my happy home, would God I were in thee! *(He stares at* KEMP *with a touch of mad challenge.)* Would God I were!

KEMP *(uncomfortable under* TYLER*'s glare and still heaving on the wheel)*: Well, would God I was too, I suppose, but –

TYLER: But! Ah! But! But, but, but . . .

KEMP *(exasperated)*: Well, we don't live in Heaven, do we?

TYLER: Do we not?

KEMP *(looks at* TYLER *and at the cart and at the sky, takes a deep breath)*: Mister Tyler. *(Looks at him like a man trying to learn a secret.)* What are you doing?

TYLER: Changing the world!

KEMP *(wrathful not at* TYLER *but at the remark)*: That's no good. What sort of an answer is that? Man, look! *(Points to the cart.)* A week ago you had a house and a job, and now . . . . Every man's hand against you, every landlord – don't think Master Richards hasn't spread the word – and where will you sleep tonight?

JOAN, *returning with the chair, hears this.*

JOAN: The Lord will give us shelter.

KEMP *(dryly)*: I hope He does it before the dew falls, Miss.

TYLER *(as if the conversation had nothing to do with him)*: As our Saviour said, 'foxes have holes and birds have nests, but the son of man has nowhere to lay his head.'

KEMP *(respectfully)*: That's Gospel, and it's Gospel truth so it is. *(a little ire)* But you're not the Saviour of the world. And what about her? She's no fox nor no nestling neither. *(Goaded by* TYLER*'s seeming complacency and genuinely concerned for* JOAN.*)* Mister, she needs a roof over her head and . . . *(He takes a deep breath.)* Excuse us Missie. *(He takes* TYLER *by the arm and moves away a few paces.* JOAN *is busy with the cart.)* Mister Tyler, it's none of my business . . .

TYLER: Say what you must so that you say the truth.

KEMP *(with genuine, simple concern)*: All right. Look, you and me, we're grown men. What happens to us is our own affair. Wait – I've heard you in Burford – yes, and I've learned something, too. We're not all like Grote, you know. But her, that lass –

TYLER: My lamb! *(aggressively)* What of her?

KEMP: Lamb! Butchers wait for them. But – *(struggling for words)* she's a girl . . . and the things she says *(overrides* TYLER*)* they may be right and they may not, but –

TYLER: More buts!

KEMP *(a little cross)*: Well life's full of them, ain't it? But that girl, reading and preaching, I'll tell you, she'll get a name as a witch.

TYLER *(mad laugh)*: Witch!

KEMP *(more cross)*: It's no laughing matter. It's been all right in Burford. Everyone knows you there, and her. But you go somewhere else . . . they drown witches, and what's going to happen to her when you've gone? *(KEMP looks in TYLER's face. Shrugs.)* Well, it's none of my affair.

TYLER *(friendly)*: Friend. *(He places his hand on KEMP's shoulder.)* I thank you for your concern, indeed I do, but . . .

His face suddenly changes from friendliness to hatred, as, over KEMP's shoulder he sees RICHARDS and PYKE enter. RICHARDS stops dead and claps his hand on a prominent pistol. KEMP turns, sees RICHARDS, and instantly backs away, doffing his hat.

RICHARDS: Keep your distance! I have a pistol!

TYLER: Aye, and a dog at your heels. Do you not have a cannon with you?

RICHARDS *(Keeping his distance,* PYKE *menacing behind him.)*: You have only yourself to blame. Those who make trouble can expect to get it.

TYLER: What trouble did I ever make? I spoke the word of God.

RICHARDS: The words of rebellion and treason. The town is well rid of you, and count yourself lucky –

TYLER points at the cart.

RICHARDS: Yes, lucky! You could be against the wall with the other agitators who are to be shot within the hour.

TYLER: And you go to see them, I suppose. It will make a fine holiday for you.

> RICHARDS *laughs contemptuously and* TYLER *explodes with anger.*

TYLER: You laugh! You dare to laugh when men are to be murdered within the hour! You drive me from my home and you laugh!

> TYLER *raises his club.* KEMP *seizes* TYLER *and pulls him back.* JOAN *joins her father.*

KEMP *(to* TYLER*)*: Calm down. *(to* RICHARDS, *apologetically)* Sorry, Sir. He's upset.

RICHARDS *(cool, knowing that* TYLER *is no danger, addresses him)*: Do as – *(stares at* KEMP*)*

KEMP *(servile)*: Kemp, Sir. Just lending a hand, Sir. *(Touches his forelock.)*

RICHARDS *(a cold, calculating gaze at* KEMP*)*: Do as Kemp tells you.

TYLER: Tells! Telling! Told! Orders!

RICHARDS: Yes, orders! Learn to obey them.

TYLER: Never while the like of you give them. Never!

RICHARDS *(coldly menacing)*: You will. You will hear and you will obey.

TYLER *(shouting defiance)*: No, *you* will hear and *you* will obey!

RICHARDS *(looks at* JOAN*)*: You are no fit father.

JOAN: None better in England.

> TYLER *and* JOAN *stand hand in hand.*

RICHARDS *(shakes his head)*: It is the end of you.

JOAN: There you are wrong.

TYLER: It is the end of you. We are but at the beginning.

RICHARDS: You are on the road to nowhere.

JOAN: We are on the road to glory.

RICHARDS: Well, well . . . . *(moved a little by the plight of* TYLER *and* JOAN*)* If you promise to be reasonable I will store your belongings until you find somewhere to live.

TYLER *now calm and collected, takes a step forward and speaks deliberately.*

TYLER: I would sooner burn them here and now.

RICHARDS: So, fanatic. Very well. Be clear of this parish by nightfall. And you –

KEMP *(frightened)*: Kemp, Sir.

RICHARDS: Kemp. Mark his name, Pyke. Be home before night.

RICHARDS *and* PYKE *exit.*

KEMP *(shame-faced; shakes the cart)*: It seems all right now. I'll have to leave you here. Its . . . I have a wife and kids, too . . .

TYLER: Friend, don't suffer on my account. We thank you for your help.

He shakes hands with KEMP.

KEMP: So, fare well.

TYLER: Wait! *(*TYLER *rummages in a box. Takes out a pamphlet.)* A gift.

KEMP *(takes the pamphlet awkwardly)*: Mister Tyler, I cannot read.

TYLER: Neither could I once. Take it.

As KEMP, *somewhat diffidently, takes the pamphlet there is a crash of musketry.* TYLER, JOAN *and* KEMP *are frozen.*

TYLER: One.

KEMP: Sweet Jesus!

Another crash of musketry.

TYLER: Two.

He sinks to his knees in prayer. JOAN *and* KEMP *join him. Lights dim on them. Opposite stage lights up. Eight men of a firing squad and a Cornet in charge. A blinded corporal (who could be* WARD*) is led out and stands, boldly.*

CORNET: Preesent! Aim!

An ominous rattle of muskets being adjusted.

CORPORAL *(shouts)*: Long live the Rev –
CORNET *(screaming him down)*: Fire!

A musket volley. The CORPORAL *slumps. Lights down on this scene. Up on* TYLER.

TYLER: Three.

All rise.

KEMP *(Shaking hands with* TYLER *and* JOAN*.)*: God go with you. I shan't forget this day.
TYLER *(kindly)*: Remember it, Brother.
KEMP: Remember me.
TYLER *(smiles)*: Remember us! Come daughter, we have a journey to make.

They move off. KEMP *watches them as they exit.*

KEMP *(shouts)*: Where are you going?
TYLER *(off-stage)*: To glory, Brother.
KEMP *(raising his arms, tempted to follow)*: To Glory!

Birds sing.

END SCENE. END ACT. END PLAY.